THE
FULATUNE
HARDINESS HANDBOOK

Also by Paul Arnault

Gheorghiu, M. D. & Arnault, P. (Eds.). (2013). *Les sciences sociales et leurs publics: engagements et distanciations*. Alexandru Ioan Cuza University Press.

THE *FULATUNE* HARDINESS HANDBOOK

Grow More Worldly-wise,
Attuned & Composed

Paul ARNAULT, M.A.

First printed in paperback in 2024

Fulatune^{SM}, *3D Worldly^{SM}*, and *3D Worldly Press^{SM}* theme names are trademarks of *3D Worldly*, EI.

ISBN-13: 978-2-487414-00-6

CONTENTS

 co

LIST OF ILLUSTRATIONS

ৎ৩

FIGURES

TABLE

PREFACE

❧

Under present circumstances, it appears that self-growth methods are mostly aimed at serving individual prosperity, social status upgrading, and happiness (at least certain conceptions of it). While our approach won't impede those goals, it was rather designed to help people become more worldly-wise, attuned, and composed. Of course, happiness is a legitimate pursuit. However, the fact that it can be achieved through illusions sometimes makes clear-eyed acumen preferable. Besides, happiness is a very personal matter, and the way you find it is, after all, none of our business. In other words, this is not a happiness manual: it's a hardiness handbook. It might at times feel uncommon or provocative as it will question conventional wisdom and discuss topics such as perception biases related to ideological, national, and cultural standpoints. Unusual acuity and disenchanting tools, such as history and sociology, will also be employed. Therefore, this preface aims to encourage readers who might not be familiar with human and social science or perhaps had a hard time in school as I sometimes did. If you encounter intricacies, you might want to: a) take a break, hang on, and consider the hardship as only temporary (instant access to dictionaries and quality sources is historically unprecedented), b) remember that skill enhancement paths are challenging by definition (hardiness acquisition is…hard), c) keep in mind that the process, as well as the outcome of effective and structured thinking, can be enjoyable and rewarding (it is, instead, rambling reflection that leads to deadlocks, sterile rumination or despair when problem-solving), and d) consider that if discovering news outlooks and concepts can be confusing at first, it will only help you, in the long run, to develop more insight and objectivity in the face of complex adversity.

INTRODUCTION

എ

Three Problems in the Mainstream Personal Development Field

A strong diversity of actors, approaches, and purposes characterizes the expanding field of personal development. On self-growth library shelves, one can find, side by side, writings from scientists popularizing evidence-based mental health research findings on anxiety and depression prevention, clerics and philosophers sharing wisdom principles on serenity, as well as self-taught entrepreneurs and military personnel advocating the virtues of determination to achieve success and leadership. Although many of these productions may differ in terms of scope or validity, they often share unquestioned frameworks and common assumptions. One example is the recurrent premise according to which ideas play a tremendous role in personal change. They certainly do. However, the external factors that support their implementation are often neglected (grants, micro-credit, emotional, medical, and technical support, political will, etc). Another example of an influential presumption is that psychology is the key discipline to understanding individual and social behavior. It is a central approach. But other disciplines such as sociology, anthropology, and even history are also significant perspectives. A last example could be the cultural bias influencing personal development. Historically and geographically, modern applied psychology and self-growth movement thrived after the First World War in the United States (Jansz and van Drunen, 2004), a country where optimism, entrepreneurship, and individualism became widespread values (Zakaras, 2022). Combined with the perspectives of idealism and psychologism, these norms have deeply shaped modern self-growth conceptions which found an international audience after the Second World War, for the better and the worse.

Personal development discourses arguably spread scientific findings and healthy encouragement on a global level. They propose numerous sensible mental health and "productivity" tips. And daily, many well-intentioned authors and speakers deliver messages of hope to millions of struggling people. The point of these comments is not to call into question the positive functions of the self-growth movement. It is to underline misdirection, shortcomings, and neglected possibilities.

Firstly, by underestimating material and social factors involved in agency and empowerment, idealistic discourses advocating voluntarism can harm people by making them believe they are entirely responsible for their misery. Mobilizing statistically rare "super-achievers" during a speech is undoubtedly inspirational and relevant given their possible merit. However, the storytelling techniques used to promote these success stories differ in accuracy and intent from in-depth biographical analysis. Besides, the (self)promoted celebrities are not the most inclined to highlight conditions that, if undisclosed, would temper their glorification (an unmentioned generous uncle, a supportive and non-dysfunctional family, an economic stimulus package, systemic privileges, etc.). One can't help to believe it would certainly be an eye-opener to research the percentage of people who have been listening to motivational speakers for 15 years or more, and who are still earning about the same income. It is also hard to believe that the 1.3 billion people living in multidimensional poverty (United Nations, 2021) simply lack the motivation to "succeed". Self-instructional techniques and coaching tips can be helpful, but detached from concrete foundations, they become naïve and ineffective solutions.

Secondly, overestimating the powers of will as a self-improvement mechanism is partly related to the idea that the origin of success primarily lies in the psychology of the individual. But individual psychology is not only a cause, it is also an effect: a product of history, social contexts, socialization, or biology. By extension, psychological primacy conceptions generally lead to social and political theories that explain collective phenomena as, essentially, the sum of individual behaviors. This bias can result in denying top-down dynamics such as systemic discrimination and preferring Bad Apple Theory types of individualistic explanation. A perfect example of political denial of collective formations and related social dynamics was given by Margaret Thatcher when she commented: "*Who is society? There is no such thing! There are individual men and women and there are families*" (Thatcher, 1987). These uninformed but influential opinions tend to worsen the fate of many people across the world (remember "Reaganomics"?). Individualism and psychologism not only overlook structural problems (racism, addiction, unemployment) but also global solutions. It is interesting to notice that the *World Health Organization*'s (WHO) *Department of Mental Health and Substance Use* experts are not advocating more individual responsibility or extra coaching tips; they are exhorting stakeholders to "*reshape the environments that influence mental health, and strengthen the systems that care for mental health*" (World Health Organization, 2022a, Back cover). British epidemiologists Richard Wilkinson and Kate Pickett established the existence of a very strong link between the role of systemic determinants in health on the one hand, and social problems on the other, which are worse in more unequal countries (Wilkinson & Pickett, 2009). Figure 1 illustrates this strong relationship. In other words, multiple behaviors, that are generally examined through the lens of individual "choices" (such as sexual, aggressive, and addictive behaviors), are heavily conditioned by social factors when analyzed from a macro-sociological perspective. As we will discuss later, our position is not to deny some degree of free will but to argue that the greater the awareness of its determinants, the more empowered it is.

Figure 1. *Health and Social Problems Are Worse in More Unequal Countries (Wilkinson & Pickett, 2009)*

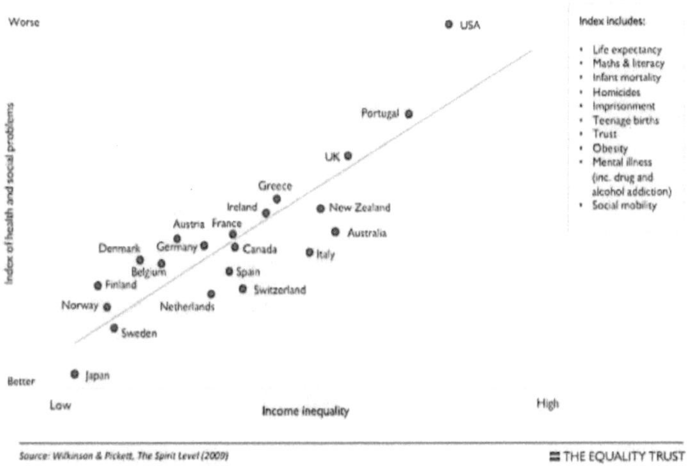

Thirdly, personal development discourses and practices are culturally biased. This fact doesn't mean it is "bad". Or "unamerican" to underline it. It simply implies that they are rooted in certain contexts and schools of thought, just like other "*technologies of the self*". According to Michel Foucault, they "*permit individuals to effect by their own means or with the help of others a certain number of operations on their own bodies and souls, thoughts, conduct, and way of being, so as to transform* [...] *themselves in order to attain a certain state of happiness, purity,*

wisdom, perfection, or immortality" (Foucault, 1988, p.18). The hegemony of American personal development discourses across the world has progressively associated the conception of success and happiness with individual material wealth, upward social mobility, leadership, and body aesthetics. The so-called American way of life has such attractiveness that it is often ironic to observe the paradoxical love and hate attitudes of many non-Americans who can simultaneously denounce real or perceived "decadence" and "imperialism" while simultaneously aspiring to enjoy the lifestyle of upper-middle-class Americans. There is also something awkward and comical, but somehow disappointing, to observe how non-American online coaches and motivational speakers across the world mimic American cheerfulness, commercial body language, and voice intonations. The cultural bias affecting the conception of "success" partly operates by selection and reduction: it selects the economic aspect of achievement and reduces it to its financial dimension. The same reductionist process affects the notion of happiness which tends to equate to social status contentment. While this wealth, performance, and dominance orientation can be endorsed by some personal development movements (human enhancement, masculinism, etc.), it is not surprising many Westerners are also disenchanted by the futility of *"the society of the spectacle"* (Debord, 1967) and have been turning (back) to mysticism or esoterism.

Knowledge and cultural biases such as idealism, individualism, psychologism, and Americanism have partly conditioned the orientation of the self-growth movement. While it is inevitable that self-care or enhancement techniques will vary according to culture, it remains preferable to keep questioning assumptions and constructively bringing up issues such as the purposes of personal development, the validity of expert claims, and professional competence.

Generally speaking, personal development experts are professionals who provide services related to self-care, social skills, and, more or less intentionally, spirituality. More or less, because unlike openly mystical movements legitimately existing within the field of personal development, such as Buddhism or shamanism, many self-growth trends simply convey plain ideology through fairly unwitting representatives. While it is understandable that certain principles such as humanism, welfare, or fulfillment are inherent to the application of human and social sciences to well-being issues, the presence of values such as "leadership", "influence", or "entrepreneurship" is questionable since they are implicitly presented as universal norms. If anthropology was promoted and popularized as much as psychology by mainstream media, people would know that. The role of psychologists, counselors, coaches, or motivational speakers is not to embody or act as ideological mouthpieces. It is to capably help their patients, clients, and audiences to cope with life's problems when they show up. What's the relationship between personal welfare and leading others anyway? The kick from a serotonin power trip? The simple satisfaction of not being the one who "follows"? Aspiring to become the leader of other rational adults somehow implies a certain depreciation of the democratic value of self-determination. And is there really a connection between entrepreneurship and serenity? If the link was that strong, there wouldn't be so many "executive coaches" out there, paid to soothe power-related stress and sometimes guilt. Besides, is it really up to behavioral experts to encourage upward social mobility, and reach managerial or moguls' positions? That is generally the role of parents and business schools. Not so long ago, a majority of CEOs seemed to have the decency to refrain from impersonating philosophers or heroes. Not so long ago, people could tell the difference between the valor of people such as Rosa Parks and the "courage" of dismissing 80% of staff in a heartbeat.

Because personal development does disseminate and vulgarize some quality science, and since motivational tips encourage people to tackle life every morning, it would be unfortunate to globally condemn the self-growth industry and throw the baby out with the bath water. But one can sometimes get the impression that personal development is tailored for people living in the world of the *"Friends"* sitcom, or that it is about positive self-talk stickers on fridges or AI-made flowery coaching templates. People are being exposed to enough vague concepts, unrealistic goals, and false promises. Moreover, too many personal development actors trespass the boundaries of simple wellness to promote bald worldviews. Worse, some motivational speakers even resort to blaming, shaming, and castigating audiences, narcissistically offering themselves as identification models. But there is every reason to believe they are confusing loudness with charisma, rhetoric with competence, and strength with solidity. What is needed is more modesty, conceptual accuracy, and clear-eyed objectivity.

Figure 2. *Example of a competency/rationality perspective applied to the self-help industry*

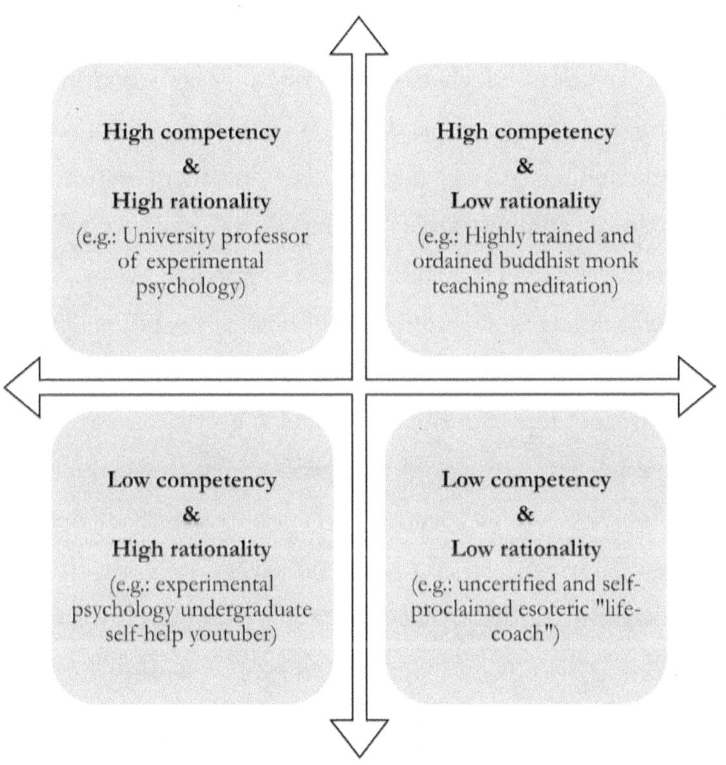

The 3D Worldly Approach and the Fulatune Training System

Personal development is not reducible to making more money, becoming powerful, or dully happy. The *3D Worldly* approach and the *Fulatune* training system were created to help people become more worldly-wise, attuned, and composed. The *Fulatune* method is mainly an applied hardiness technique. Hardiness is defined by the *American Psychological Association* (APA) as: "*the ability to adapt easily to unexpected changes combined with a sense of purpose in daily life and of personal control over what occurs in one's life*" (APA, 2018)[1].

Adaptation, which is in fact rarely "easy", is necessary to most enterprises and starts with observation and understanding the goal-related environment (corporate, academic, administrative, political, associative, athletic, military, etc.). The *3D Worldly* approach is rational, multidisciplinary, integrative, and holistic. It is rational in the sense that it complies with scientific and logical reasoning and procedures. It is open to good faith discussion and is refutable. It is rational by not resorting to unaccountable, specious, or mystical arguments. As an element of applied human sciences, it contains standards such as "truth", "humanism", "benevolence" or "welfare". However, it remains vigilant regarding political, economic, or ideological influences. Its rationality doesn't necessarily discard the

---

1   For a pioneering scientific study, see Kobasa (1979).

positive effects of mysticism and ideology on motivation, courage, hope, and self-efficacy (it doesn't turn a blind eye to the negative either). It simply sticks to the scientific position that all phenomena have (or can have) a rational explanation. The *3D Worldly* approach is multidisciplinary in the sense that it makes use, not only of psychology, but also of history, sociology, anthropology, political science, and biology to shed light on behaviors and situations. Why history? Because there might be 400 years beneath a refusal to smile back, not just a personality trait or a simple mood disorder. The approach is not advocating the abolition of disciplinary boundaries, it only intends to further integrate perspectives whose disciples sometimes barely even discuss with each other anymore. It doesn't only rely on theoretical perspectives: it also draws upon practical knowledge, matured from durable exposure to challenging real-life situations, such as street smarts, tradecraft, and strategy. Lastly, the *3D Worldly* approach defends an integral biopsychosocial outlook to the understanding of behavior and situations.

The *Fulatune* training system is the more practical side of the *3D Worldly* approach. It actualizes its attributes and principles by organizing them into building blocks foundations, procedural steps, and training programs. While many systems start by idealistically exhorting audiences to initiate change by modifying their cognitions, the *Fulatune* method only considers that phase to be most effective when physiological and sociological conditions are met. It aims at developing worldliness, adaptation, and composure by proposing to follow three stages: observation, understanding, and adaptation (OUA). Many models skip the observation phase, naïvely succumbing to the empiricist fallacy consisting of regarding perceptions as an undistorted reflection of external reality. The fact is that perceptions about oneself and the world are distorted and shaped by many factors: ideology, social structures, social status and mobility, cultural and subcultural environments, socialization, gender, ethnicity, stereotypes, trends, assumptions, education, personality type, coping mechanisms, cognitive biases, etc. This primer will discuss ways to better control these effects. Once the act of observing has been monitored, understanding has a better chance of being accurate. However, the act of understanding a behavior or situation is also exposed to deformed impacts such as overlooked biases and diverse interpretation frameworks. Understanding accurately if not correctly a behavior or situation not only implies having frameworks (generally a main one) but also acknowledging their existence and possible effects. It is even more beneficial to have knowledge of the frames other people are utilizing in a given situation and to know how they might shape their thinking and acting. Negotiating a compromise at the United Nations or a family dinner table is best done with the proper tools and skills. Once accurate observation and interpretation have been accomplished, conditions are improved for optimal adaptation and action. Most purposes in life involve road maps that require strategies and actions involving physiological, cognitive, emotional, and behavioral adaptations. We would like to make clear that adaptation is not considered here as a virtue or a social necessity. Many historical examples illustrate why it is sometimes important to refuse to adapt and comply. But sometimes you need to adapt because job choices are limited in the area. Or you wish to because belonging to that group would be so gratifying. This primer offers advice on reasons and ways to adapt to adverse situations as well as the general principles, mechanisms, steps, and applications of the *Fulatune* method

Figure 3. *Relationships between the 3D Worldly approach and the Fulatune training method*

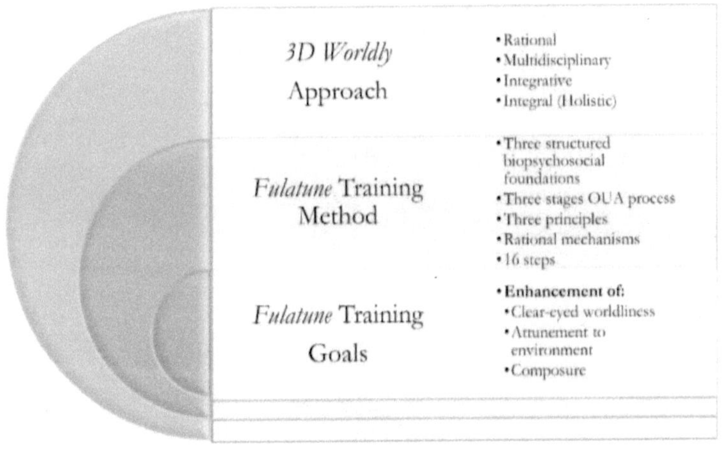

PART I
Three Foundations
& Three Stages

Within the pedagogical community, two main ways of teaching exist: the first one is generally called "deductive" (from theory to practice), and the other "inductive" (from practice to theory). There is a consensus concerning the necessity of prioritizing and sticking to the inductive method with students who struggle with grades. I strongly disagree with that premise. Because I am convinced it is partly based on class prejudice: some (often the same) would be too dumb to understand abstract ideas. One of the problems is that many students end up interiorizing that belief and, as a result, start requesting that learning contents be oversimplified, thus creating a downward spiral fulfilling the initial idiocy prophecy. *"Do to understand"* is an implicit motto for many teachers. Why not? Occasionally. But giving up on the objective of *"thinking to understand"* is unacceptable, especially for a pedagogue. One needs to alternate methods when necessary, not dogmatically cling to only one. I also enjoy easy-to-understand ideas and tangible explanations; I therefore use many concrete examples to illustrate notions. However, I will unapologetically use concepts and refuse to comply with the marketing-distorted syntax checker inviting me to be more "concise". Some complex phenomena, such as… human affairs for instance, require time, patience, nuances, and adverbs. Not bullet-point memorizing.

The objective of this first part is not to convince you through pathos; it is to display how the *Fulatune* method was conceived and why it was built that way, so you understand the reasons behind the principles and steps presented in the second part of the book. Chapter one deals with biopsychosocial foundations. It stresses the importance of "paving the way" to the adaptation process. Chapter two is about the importance of observing before analyzing. While observations are often already actual analyses (because of frameworks such as stereotypes), it remains essential to recognize the difference between perception and interpretation. Chapter three concerns understanding. It presents many levels and ways of grasping internal and external reality. Chapter 4 critically discusses the concept of adaptation, its different purposes and means.

CHAPTER 1
Biopsychosocial Foundations

❧

The *Fulatune* method emphasizes the usefulness of well-prepared social problem-solving activities. There are of course advantages in just jumping into action: one gains time from the start, avoids the discomfort of mental and emotional anticipation, and can tackle the successive challenges later, when they show up. But the time gained in the early stages of problem-solving can be lost during the following ones because such or such factor was neglected. And short-circuiting the disturbance implied in preparation will most certainly be costly in terms of composure when facing a challenge that could have been met with more serenity if foreseen. Ultimately, dealing with problems only when they appear has a major inconvenience: having to go through a decision-making phase that could have been shortened by preliminary "if, then" options. In certain social situations, even a split-second hesitation can shuffle the cards in favor of the opposition.

This approach advocates putting the problem of preparation on its head by building foundations on three successive levels: physiological, sociological, and then, psychological. Firstly, it involves consolidating physiological and physical conditions first, if feasible (basically: sleep, hydration, and nutrition). For example, low blood sugar levels are not a good start for social interaction, positive self-talk, or optimistic outlooks. Secondly, it advises mobilizing, as much as possible, social resources such as technical and emotional support before goal-driven action. Of course, a boxer is alone in the ring when facing his opponent. But the interiorized technical and emotional support provided by his team carries to some extent his psychology. Thirdly, once these two requirements are fulfilled, the implementation of previously learned cognitive and behavioral techniques is encouraged.

Figure 4. *Biopsychosocial foundational disposition of the* Fulatune *method*

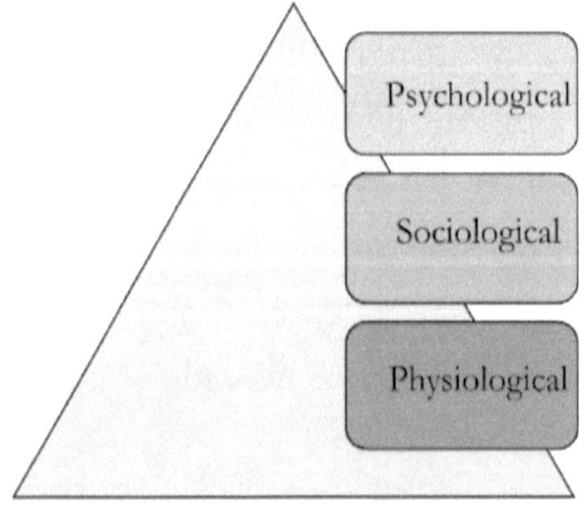

1.1. Physiological and Physical Health Foundations

We acknowledge that what breakfast researchers call "skippers" often say they are perfectly fine, and we recognize that intermittent fasting suits some people. Nonetheless, the evidence tends to indicate that performance tasks are generally higher when physiological needs such as hydration (Masento et al., 2014) and nutrition are met. The same goes for lack of sleep: the negative effects of fatigue on cognition, mood, and social relationships are well known today (National Health Service, 2020). All things being equal, sufficient hydration, nutrition, and sleep are better for optimal psychological and social functioning.

Physical activity represents another foundation of health. But all the ideological chatter about the hardcore "no excuse" workouts invites us to clarify the limits of training advantages. The WHO indicates that, in general, adults (18-64 years old) *"should do at least 150–300 minutes of moderate-intensity aerobic physical activity, or at least 75–150 minutes of vigorous-intensity aerobic physical activity; or an equivalent combination of moderate- and vigorous-intensity activity throughout the week"* (World Health Organization, 2022b). It adds that they *"may increase moderate-intensity aerobic physical activity to more than 300 minutes; or do more than 150 minutes of vigorous-intensity aerobic physical activity; or an equivalent combination of moderate and vigorous-intensity activity throughout the week for additional health benefits."* (WHO, 2022). The organization also mentions that, on the one hand, physical activity reduces symptoms of depression and anxiety, and on the other hand, it enhances thinking, learning, and judgment skills (WHO, 2022). The positive health effects of moderate exercise on the immune system are known, but when practiced at intensive levels it can cause an increase in health problems such as infections (O'Kennedy, 2000). Heavy exercise sessions, involving the self-control to endure potentially painful and/or exhausting efforts, can also provoke willpower depletion (Baumeister & Tierney, 2011), willpower being *"the ability to delay gratification, resisting short-term temptations in order to meet long-term goals"* (APA, 2022). Questions can be raised when people start to "need" their daily super-dose of exercise just to feel operational. Even though the hours spent exercising might seem psychologically worth it in terms of sharpness or self-esteem, one can raise questions. Could they represent a waste of time and energy? Could exercising a lot be an activism defense mechanism destined to mask nagging thoughts/ feelings (like running… away), or travestying procrastination as well spent time? Could training or practicing that much objectify peer-pressure effect (holy glutes), or excessive conformity to mundane trends despite a cool maverick self-concept (supposedly badass tattoos)? Wouldn't it be more useful for psychological well-being and social fulfillment to take 4 hours out of the PT weekly program to, instead, put them into other activities such as education, skills development, or artistic practice?

1.2. Sociological Foundations

To put it mildly, personal development narratives do not usually start by underlining the importance of sociological factors in psychological health. The individualistic bias in self-growth programs masks the social conditions requested for people to enhance their well-being, such as public street workout equipment or laws condemning workplace bullying[2]. It is difficult for people to develop emotional well-being if their environment is ridden by violence, addiction, promiscuity, or unemployment. At the macro-sociological level, these environments can generate widely shared stress, hopelessness, and trauma. People who overcame social adversity can of course be a source of inspiration to many. But self-made men's or women's success stories can also stigmatize the majority who are struggling. Firstly, serious investigation into "great" individual trajectories can reveal a few more hidden advantages than hagiographic biographies evoke. Secondly, one cannot logically recognize the existence of systemic injustice, and, simultaneously, deny structural determinism when it suits their personal storytelling needs.

It is often very difficult to bypass unfavorable social conditions such as a rough neighborhood, a homophobic town, or a dysfunctional family. If breaking away can be the only solution to maintain minimal mental health or protect

---

2   Practicing "assertiveness" won't always save you from corporate harassment and it doesn't work universally: you will come across as impolite in many non-Western cultures.

children from gang socialization, the move isn't given to everyone. Of course, individuals play a fundamental role in their psychosocial well-being. But too often, this role is reduced to an entirely personal action such as altering a "mindset" or making a life-changing "decision". Things are a bit more complicated. Social conditions are necessary for efficient change: some circumstances must sometimes be combined to leave an abusive partner (such as a steady job, a helping family member, a local refuge guaranteeing secrecy of location to avoid retaliation, etc.). To engage in sobriety, you might need minimal financial stability and a support network, a wake-up call such as the legal warning that you might lose the custody of a child, or at least a few viable alternatives to drinking yourself to death. In addition to your goodwill and ambition, the *State Small Business Credit Initiative* or some "love money" might be necessary to make your business dream come true. It follows that an individual will be better off if he works on consolidating social conditions *before* chanting morning motivational mantras in front of the mirror (one could do both at the same time though).

1.3. Psychological Foundations

When physiological and sociological conditions are taken care of, it is easier to work on psychological conditions (we will talk about psychological *techniques* later). For example, it is easier to "put yourself in the mood" for some specific goal-related action if you are no longer on an empty stomach or caught up in sick family dynamics. This is pretty much what we mean when we talk about "psychological conditions".

Before tackling an issue, problem-solving therapy pioneers such as Thomas D'Zurilla and Marvin Goldfried (D'Zurilla & Goldfried,1971) and Arthur Nezu (Nezu & D'Zurilla, 1979) discovered that taking the time to work on the attitude toward the activity of problem-solving was a decisive factor in the success of the therapy. Many counselors skip this fundamental step to jump right into the analysis of the problem (why is the person consulting? What is their problem?). If individuals are identified as having "negative problem orientation" (as opposed to "positive problem orientation"), the therapist would be well advised to take some time to work on beliefs concerning the general solvability of problems and the perception that patients or clients have regarding their ability to solve problems: "*Negative problem orientation has been defined as a disruptive cognitive-emotional set, or attitude, toward problems that includes perceived threat of problems to well-being, self-inefficacy or doubt over one's problem-solving ability, the tendency to be pessimistic about the outcome, and low frustration tolerance. Positive problem orientation, on the other hand, has been described as a constructive cognitive set reflecting perceived challenge, self-efficacy, and positive outcome expectancy."* (Robichaud & Dugas, 2005, p. 391). The counselor will also determine which "problem-solving style" people generally use. Decades of research have revealed three significant categories: a) rational or planful, b) impulsive/careless, and c) avoidant. From the standpoint of goal attainment objectives, it is preferable to make these tendencies clear to individuals so they can eventually work on them before engaging in problem-solving or goal-orientated activities. Not doing it is potentially time costly and project jeopardizing.

A steadied body, emotional and technical support, and positive problem orientation are an optimal combination to start real-life problem-solving actions. Sometimes, you will lack one or the other and will have to rely solely on psychological techniques to maintain or boost morale and make decisions. Occasionally, you will be literally on your own to face adversity, because your situation doesn't fit into bureaucratic categories, or because your family and friends united to chorus: *"Money's too tight to mention"* (The Valentine Brothers, 1982). You might also be too proud to ask for help, which is understandable. There is often a great degree of naïveté in thinking it's easy to just "reach out" and that no power dynamics come into play in assistance situations. This is why it is important to work upstream on problem orientation, cognitive distortions, and relaxation techniques. Starting to practice cognitive restructuring or meditation when things are already bad is a little late because managing these skills takes years. Mastering them will maximize the chances of buffering the negative effects of nutritional depletion and lack of resources and support. Since many online resources now present cognitive distortions as well as ways to manage them, we will not develop these common knowledge points here. While this primer does mention them, its purpose is to focus on the new *Fulatune* method based on three sequences of actions: observation, understanding, and adaptation.

CHAPTER 2
Step 1: Observation

❧

"To watch carefully especially with attention to details or behavior for the purpose of arriving at a judgment"
Merriam-Webster

Observing represents the first step in grasping external and internal reality. Yet, the observation act is often biased by beliefs and other distortions. It can also be plainly skipped (*"jumping to conclusions"*). One of them, found in and outside the scientific community, is naïve empiricism, or the idea according to which it is possible to simply record data without prejudice. It is commonly believed that observation is a neutral act of pure perception. And in a sense, that is true: everybody can observe an individual walking in a waiting room in a similar manner. In another, observation is already a socially constructed view. For example, if a woman walks into a waiting room, everybody will perceive the same image, but individuals can spontaneously make very different observations according to their perception frameworks:

-*"Looks like a good soul"*

-*"Great, one more coming to spread germs"*

-*"Bet she's got Medicaid"*

-*"Hooo, not bad…"*

-Etc.

There is also a tendency to perceive things globally or holistically. This proclivity is often very useful in daily life but can fail to seize fundamental details that could alter the significance of the whole. As the Austrian philosopher Christian von Ehrenfels theorized in 1890, we often tend to perceive things as a whole rather than by adding up elements (Ash, 1995). For example, even if a clerk (impolitely) scans a person walking in the store, he'll fabricate a global impression without really having to cumulate data such as: "chukka boots" + "ordinary bootcut jeans" + badly cut T-shirt" + "mid-range *Casio*" + "unimaginative tattoo" + "long forearms hair" + "lumpish posture" + "outdated soul patch" + "gullible expression" + "home-made haircut" = "not bankable". Holistic appraisals are not good or bad: they can be very valuable if one is experienced (say, to intuitively detect conmen) but they can be misleading: by definition, they leave potentially important information out (level of wit, education, etc.).

We also tend to classify too quickly. Classes depend significantly on the observers' categories of perception. The above clerk could be a lower-middle class part-time clothes salesperson aspiring to become a freelance stylist and is perhaps snobbishly overestimating his or her "good taste". The tendency to categorize is common to animals (predator/ prey, edible/inedible, etc.) but humans have developed the ability to suspend judgment, to a certain degree. Why not use that faculty more often? In general, we use a lot of biased and stereotypical thinking. While it can be vital to interpret a phenomenon in a split second (military "friend or foe" guess), it is generally unnecessary. Therefore, if the act is not too neurotically lengthy, taking time to observe before jumping to conclusions or into action is usually more advantageous. It is also challenging since it requires minimal self-regulation capabilities.

Biases of perception also affect how we relate to our inner reality. The popularity of Paul Ekman's research on the universal character of a few basic emotional facial expressions shouldn't overshadow the fact that these same emotions are culturally codified. A particular emotion can be sensed in different manners according to cultural settings. For example, shame can be felt differently in Japan and in the United States where expressions such as *"Do you own thing"*, *"what do you care?!"* or *"Let it all hang out"* are quite common and linked to values such as individualism. Fear or pain can be accepted differently by a farmer and a poet, according to different conceptions of masculinity. Sexual desire is also conditioned diversly across the world (no examples needed here). Because perceptions are also socially constructed, sharp observation skills need to encompass consciousness about how one's internal and external senses are shaped by social class, gender, ethnicity, ideology, culture, or history. Acknowledging how our sensations and perceptions are influenced by these factors or, as we mentioned earlier, fatigue or hunger, helps us control distortions that can lead to misinterpretations, inadequate reactions, or unhelpful behaviors.

2.1. Observation Skills Can Be Enhanced

Even though remarkable observation skills can be possessed by someone who has keen practical knowledge of life matters but no academic education, it makes little doubt that the same individual would benefit from human and social science knowledge. In other words, there is no way around it: reinforcing observation skills comes with learning. It also comes from practicing. An untrained observer might see the same scene as a shrewd one but will more likely be blind to some aspects of it. A skilled (and willing) observer will not just notice the dressing style, the type of glasses, or the presence of a ring worn by the woman walking in the waiting room. He or she will pick up more subtle sociological and psychological indicators that can generate meaning when combined, such as the carriage, gait, amount of make-up, the space monopolized by the gestures, greeting style, voice clarity and volume, diction, way of looking at others, expression of the mouth, quality of cloth dye and fabric, chromatic tones and combination, etc. Observation can extend to environmental characteristics such as the volume and proprieties of decoration in the room, the standing of furniture, the type and shape of magazines lying on the table, the smell and level of oxygenation, types of sociolinguistic markers emanating from the interactions at the secretary's desk, etc.

Few groups benefit from training that develops extended observation skills in real-life settings. Amongst the better-equipped ones stand anthropologists, sociologists, social psychologists but also case officers. Of course, clinical psychologists and psychiatrists are competent observers, but it is our experience that many are prone to overlook sociological behavioral influences and tend to mistake them for individual characteristics, which constitutes a serious interpretation error. For different reasons, some novelists, politicians, and criminals are quite accomplished observers too.

2.2. Observation Needs Frameworks

Unless it is crucial to make an immediate decision (brake, duck, smile back, avoid eye contact, shoot, etc.), it is wise to stay in the observation phase for a while and suspend judgment. The attitude of mindfulness during meditation or the technique of *"evenly suspended attention"* psychoanalysts' employ are, to a certain extent, examples of a mindset that lets internal or external information unfold freely without attaching special interest to any particular element. But while the meditator is not looking for anything, other observers are vaguely looking for something: a manifestation of the unconscious such as a slip for the analyst, "suspicious activity" for a law enforcement agent (the activity is often ambiguous in the beginning), a non-verbal flirting clue for someone who wants to develop a relationship with a potential partner that could have seemed out of reach so far, etc.

The intention of looking for "something" indicates the existence of some kind of framework created to discriminate and receive certain types of data. Facts need frames to purvey meaning. Frameworks are necessary after the observation but also before: what at you looking for? How are you going to select relevant information? Imagine you are standing on a platform in a huge train station and observing a buzzing crowd. If you don't segment your observation, you won't have much to say except: *"I see a bunch of folks walking"* or *"That's a fidgeting throng"*. You can clarify the shuffle by creating perception categories and questions. Are blonds the majority? What is the dominant color worn? Do men walk faster than women? Is "business casual" the main dress style? Who's acting differently than the majority? Who could the pickpockets be? Does anybody look lost? Who looks like a veteran traveler? The questions are mainly determined by the identity of the observer (beggar, policeman, pickpocket, or pickup "artist"). They are also determined by motives (accumulating coins and why not bills, spotting seemingly weak and distracted prey, reducing petty theft and/or meeting quota standards, etc.) and hypotheses based on experience or stereotypes: naïve looking young people dressed in a bohemian style are more generous than hurried people dressed in formal office wear, drug dealers choose regular and specific selling spots in the station, easy prey gather around the information booth, etc.

At this stage, there is no real explanation or understanding yet, although observers benefiting from decades of theoretical and practical experience can observe, explain, and understand behavior and situations almost instantaneously given their highly attuned practical sense. But explaining and understanding come after perception, and, generally, the more accurate the perception, the better the appreciation.

CHAPTER 3
Step 2: Understanding

ↄ

*"To achieve a grasp of the nature,
significance, or explanation of something"*
Merriam-Webster

Commonly, observations are shallow because they are not grounded in interest, in both senses of curiosity and/or benefit. The analysis is maintained to a minimum, and information is lazily treated in binary categories, through the shortest neural pathway (useful/useless, good/bad, pleasant/unpleasant, new/old, sexy/unsexy, etc.). Processing that follows this type of quick filtering is already compromised. Quick-to-judge people can impress some audiences with their "got-it-all-figured-out" overconfidence, but in reality, their flash-type decision-making will often lead to negative consequences such as lopsided reasoning, damaged relationships, or physical injury. On the other hand, some people can also get stuck in neverending observations and analyses for different reasons (neurotic condition, chronic intoxication, lack of framework or method). If some assessment is better than none, inaction can be as ineffective and detrimental as impulsiveness if it doesn't follow a deliberate wait-and-see strategy. It is difficult to commit to Henri Bergson's 1937 motto and be able to act as a person of thought and think as a person of action (Bergson, 1972).

Understanding real-life situations and problems requires interpretation tools. This doesn't mean that these instruments all need to be acquired in school. It doesn't imply either that utensils solely acquired through personal experience (and anti-intellectual prejudice) are better. A combination of academic knowledge and street smarts, for example, is always better than only one or the other skill. Indeed, if you are freshly hired and "invited" to a work gathering, your education will help you understand the technicalities of some manager's discourse while your street smarts can tune your intuition to guard against a slimy colleague. The time you paused to observe the room before entering the dense and complex network of social relations (instead of naively diving into the configuration) will surely have given you some preliminary information on the people and clans in attendance. Since this is not a careerism handbook, let's say your goal is, at this point, to just understand the dynamics and stakes at play without alienating too many decision-makers with your Western assertiveness or "radical honesty". Observation probably won't yet uncover the virtuous, the self-reliant, the trustworthy, the psychopaths, or the truly powerful; but you could already spot the sycophants, the misfits, or the ostracized. It is important, though, to remember that impressions are merely hypotheses that will need further testing. Keeping an open mind is often uncomfortable because it leaves you in a state of uncertainty. But if your goal is to come close to accuracy, or even the truth, patience and flexibility are good allies: sooner or later, confirmation or refutation usually comes.

This chapter is divided into two main sections. The first one (3.1) concerns the problem of overcoming multiple obstacles to accurate understanding. It presents some attitudes, biases, and distortions that tend to bend and shape internal and external reality. The second one (3.2) deals with the more positive acts of understanding and explaining. It displays various factors, often underrated, that partly and jointly determine behaviors. It then evokes critical thinking tools that contribute to solid reasoning.

3.1. Understanding How and Why Interpretations Can Go Wrong

Misguided interpretations can ruin the efforts deployed in the observation phase. So understanding how and why interpretations can be biased is at least as important as knowing how they can be as accurate as possible. One fundamental factor in accurate understanding is the acknowledgment of partial ignorance and incompetence. This attitude of modesty is uncommon in general but also, in particular, when it comes to learning knowledge concerning philosophy or human sciences. If people can easily admit incompetence in matters of chemistry, mathematics, or microbiology (with some exceptions such as the anti-Covid bleach injection presidential idea), they tend to be more reluctant to concede their limits in the realm of sociology, psychology, or philosophy. It seems that the relative capacity to observe and understand human behavior authorizes many media or bar commentators to believe they essentially figured out the main principles of social dynamics, human motives, as well as the meaning of life. This phenomenon often leads to the apparent defeat of reason by rhetoric.

3.1.1. Understanding and Modesty

> *"For I was conscious that I knew practically nothing"*
> Socrates (as cited by Plato)

Admitting that our pretensions and preconceptions might be obstacles to understanding is an important step in the learning process. This accepting attitude is grounded in the admission that frameworks shape our understanding. And modesty implies prudence before invoking general "laws" or "rules" (rather than tendencies) and making unilateral assumptions concerning human nature (greed, dominance, heterosexuality, etc.), group characteristics (stinginess, industriousness, laziness), or historical mechanisms (progress, modernization, revolution, decadence). Uncertainty and ambiguity are often uncomfortable. Some of the most advanced theoretical works in history and social science have underlined the unpredictable and contingent nature of history (Sewell, 2005). It also takes modesty to acknowledge that we simply "don't know". However, states of perplexity are partly temporary because they are inherent to a process aimed at deciding a satisfactory course of action. Evading the discomforting feeling by quick action can end up in experiencing the long-lasting bitterness of hasty decision-making (unemployment, incarceration, paralysis, war, etc.).

3.1.2. Knowing and Controlling Biases Through Metacognition and Learning

Reducing the probabilities of flawed interpretations implies not only the awareness of deformative influences but also the capability to control them. The now popular "cognitive distortions" clinical psychology concept has helped many people to develop metacognition which *"refers to awareness of one's cognitive processes, including examining own biases and decision making"* (Szczepanik et al., 2020, para. 1). However other overarching biases, studied by social psychologists, sociologists, historians, and philosophers are not as well known.

Rising above the simple individual cognitive distortion level and gaining height by understanding more general forces is crucial to developing real acumen. Among these swaying phenomena are general knowledge biases, voguish behavioral models, cognitive biases and heuristics[3], cognitive distortions, and defense mechanisms.

---

3   The concept of "heuristics" will be presented in part 3.1.2.3.

Figure 5. *Bias reduction process*

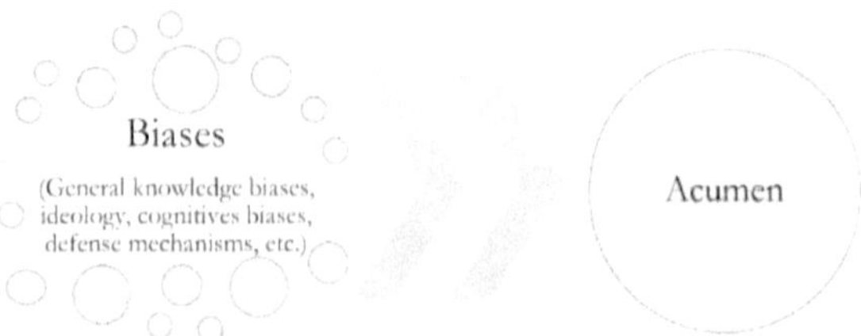

3.1.2.1. General Knowledge Biases

One of the most invisible frameworks that shape our understanding is historical "mentalities". For historians, mentalities are a set of beliefs, attitudes, values, and thinking models shared by people who lived during a particular historical period or belonged to a specific cultural group. A few comments on history need to be made here. In general, audiences easily accept the idea that our ancestors were in great part mystified by magical beliefs, feudal ideologies or influenced by false ideas. We know so much more now, don't we? It even feels good to finally be so knowledgeable. But just like our ancestors, we are still exposed to distortive ideologies (authoritarianism, libertarianism, nationalism, etc.) and false beliefs (earth being flat, immigration being the main cause of delinquency, violence being consubstantial to Islam, etc.). We too will figure in future school history (electronic) handbooks (or audiobooks if we can't read anymore) as being quite ignorant and impressionable.

Perhaps pictures illustrating the era started in the 1980s will show families watching reality TV, adults playing at crushing virtual candies or humans, and ecstatic supporters yelling at chauvinist political rallies.

For students who haven't chosen to learn history, historical reflection can generate as much enthusiasm as the invitation to watch a black-and-white movie (even a masterpiece). History appears useless, perhaps even more so in utilitarian and pragmatist cultures. Introductory courses that historicize topics can curiously generate deep disbelief and even, strangely, very strong feelings such as anger: the "usefulness" of history is simply inconceivable at first. This socially constructed attitude is a serious problem. For example, in the United States, *"63 percent of Millennials and Gen Z did not know six million Jews were murdered"* by the Nazis (CLAIMS Conference, 2020, para. 9). One could only imagine statistics in a few years if the *"Black History Month"* was somehow canceled. Among the many reasons why history is not that popular is, perhaps, the fact that it isn't as lucrative as applied psychology, neuroscience, or economics (try finding a history consultancy firm…). Personal development experts are more concerned with the future. That's understandable. Nevertheless, a little historical analysis now and then could help answer questions such as how "technologies of the self" basically turned into economic growth tools or new-age religions.

Overarching biases are hard to detect despite (and because) of their ubiquity. We have mentioned idealism and psychologism, but others are dangerously revived, such as biologism (overestimating the role of biology and heredity in human cognitive and social activity, such as intelligence or deviance) and essentialism (believing that certain group attributes are permanent and possess fixed traits, like work ethic or athleticism). Biological psychology, but also social cohesion, were severely damaged when psychologist Richard J. Herrnstein and political scientist Charles Murray strangely examined causalities and came up with a twisted interpretation of IQ distributions in the US: economic disparities between ethnicities were, in their view, partly determined by genetic differences in terms of intelligence (Herrnstein and Murray, 1994). Hopefully, inter-disciplinary cooperation and the development of epigenetic mechanisms studies will reduce the risk of this type of work seeing the light of day too often. Epigenetic mechanisms *"have been proposed as the means by which environmental and psychosocial factors such as toxins and early childhood experiences interact with physiology: They affect neural function through changes in gene expression that lead to individual differences in cognition and behavior (e.g., learning, memory, aggression, affect)."* (APA, 2023).

Within the scientific community, other biases continue to characterize understanding, often but not always along disciplinary lines, such as idealism or naïve empiricism. A specific one was coined the "scholastic bias" (*biais scholastique*) by sociologist Pierre Bourdieu (Bourdieu, 2000), who borrowed the expression "scholastic view" from John Austin (Austin, 1976). One of the meanings of "scholastic bias" is the tendency for scholars, who usually work in privileged and distanced social settings, to mistake the models they elaborate to understand behavior for the principles according to which people behave in reality This can be a tricky idea to grasp so let's use an example: a criminologist applying a rational action framework will tend to think that crime-committing deviants act as they do because they primarily use a cost-benefit model and compare the advantages of the imagined infraction with the time they could spend in prison for perpetrating it. That aspect of the behavioral explanation represents a form of legalistic bias that neglects other factors such as early deviant socialization, values, honor determinants, or community unemployment rates.

Working within disciplinary frameworks can of course foster certain biases in the study of behavior. Anthropologists can fall into culturalism (overestimating the influence of culture or norms on behavior and overlooking other factors such as economy and politics), sociologists into sociologism (overestimating social determinism and overemphasizing macro-level analysis, overlooking the study of self-determination, agency, and interaction), psychologists into psychologism (underestimating social determinism, neglecting macro-level analysis and overestimating free will and choice), biologists into biologism (overestimating genetic factors while neglecting social and psychological factors governing conduct). Nevertheless, truly erudite scholars (like Austin and Bourdieu) or have a fair knowledge of how their colleagues from other disciplines work (like science studies experts) are better equipped to, at least in part, circumvent this tendency.

3.1.2.2. *Trendy and Misleading Behavioral Models*

Just like haircuts, behavioral theories go in and out of fashion. The ones that are popular today might be looked at with scorn and derision in a generation (which doesn't necessarily mean they are invalid). And vice-versa. One of the most popular modes of behavioral explanation today is rational action theory derivatives that overestimate the role of conscious calculation in conduct: life would be a sum of conscious "choices". Of course, cost-benefit estimation is a common factor involved in acting. We do make calculated choices. However, many behaviors are still driven by the allegiance to traditional customs. Tradition remains a strong determinant for, say, Mormons, royal families, tribes, etc. Max Weber coined the term "traditional action" to designate action motives related to obedience to traditional norms. Individuals can also deploy what he called "Value-Rational Action" that can go against one's interest (avoiding physical harm) or traditional dogma (heterosexual norm, etc.). For example, not so long ago, people had second thoughts before shamelessly accepting to become human billboards on social media.

Another popular approach stems from evolutionary psychology that developed sharply in the 1990s: many cognitive mechanisms, emotions, and social behaviors may be the product of natural selection. By procuring advantages, some psychological traits were conserved. This main hypothesis makes sense. So much sense that not a day goes by without thousands of online justifications on how this or that type of behavior was useful to our ancestors, therefore… good, and even virtuous. By naturalizing behaviors such as buying testosterone precursor supplements, choosing a bodybuilder for a mate, or spending an hour a day on make-up, this bias evacuates other behavioral determinants (cultural, social, economic, etc.).

Other biases are common in contemporary babble concerning relationships and dating issues: biologism and essentialism. Hundreds of podcasters are making use of (and deforming) evolutionary psychology to justify a conservative and naturalistic conception of masculinity. In their view, men should be as virile, domineering, bustling, muscular, and libidinous as possible. This shallow philosophy of strength assumes that "alpha males" are indispensable to species survival and that heterosexual women love it even when they claim they don't. These podcasters forget that masculinity models change and that many heterosexual women would still prefer Marvin Gaye or Cary Grant over a brawny poker face action movie star.

As we underlined in the introduction, many personal development narratives are framed by culturally biased idealism, psychologism, and individualism that deeply impregnate conceptions of fulfillment. A core self-growth premise is that most individuals can transcend major socio-environmental factors through willpower. This assumption is often based on associated essentialism, in the sense that it is believed that some kind of vague pre-existing force has been there from the start and that it is just waiting to be unbound by some kind of awakening initiative. If "success" was primarily determined by the voluntary uncaging of mysterious energy existing in everybody, statistical relationships between income on the one hand, and social origin, ethnicity, nationality, or gender on the other would be inexistent. Sociology can be a real killjoy. Some basic elements of neuroscience have become so popular nowadays ("hormones", "neurotransmitters", "pathways", etc.) that hearing comments such as *"Oh, he's just hooked on dopamine, you shouldn't overthink his behavior"* or *"she's hardwired that way, don't sweat it"* has become banal. Who needs to be thanked for creating such a penetrating and curious generation of vloggers and screenwriters?

3.1.2.3. *Cognitive Biases and Heuristics*

Cognitive experts have studied how human judgments can be impaired[4]. The study of cognitive biases involved in interpreting human behavior and situations has led to the identification of certain tendencies. A few can be briefly presented here. The *Fundamental attribution error* consists of neglecting environmental factors in the understanding of other people's conduct while overemphasizing internal factors such as heredity or character. How convenient, we'll tend to think of external factors when explaining ours (*Actor-observer bias*). *Self-serving bias* is the proneness to attribute negative outcomes to environmental factors but positive ones to personal attributes such as intelligence or willpower. Commonly, people also tend to neglect intermediate or nuanced possibilities when perceiving a situation, leading to think it can only unfold in two ways (*False dichotomy*). Also very frequent is the *Confirmation bias* consisting of looking for and favoring information that will tend to confirm already made opinions and neglecting data that contradicts it. When trying to understand situations, people tend to be sensitive to the way information is "framed" or presented to us (*Framing bias*). But we cherish the thought that we have solid self-determination, even though we strongly tend to hold opinions and behave a certain way because the majority holds them (*Bandwagon effect*). More easily than what we'd like to think, we also switch opinions to conform our ideas and behavior to match the ones of the majority (*Conformity bias*)

---

4   See, for example: Baron, J. (2008). *Thinking and deciding* (4th ed.). Cambridge University Press.

or comply with the commands of people who have or seem to have authority, even if the compliance involves behaviors that are contrary to our standards (*Authority obedience bias*). This bias is a little different than the simple *Authority bias* that compels people to trust powerful people or experts without always discussing their assertions. Concerning true or imagined competence, psychologists have proposed that people with relatively low ability in a given domain tend to overestimate their skills (*Dunning-Kruger effect*). Another reassuring proneness: the probability of intervening in a situation where somebody is in danger is lower if other people are present; it also tends to decrease as the number of people present at the scene increases (*Bystander effect*).

Heuristics, derived from the Greek word *"heuriskein"* ("to discover", "to find") are generally described as "mental shortcuts" people use to make decisions under uncertainty. Although heuristics can lead to biases, they can be useful when quick decisions are necessary. Three main heuristics have been presented by psychologists Amos Tversky and Daniel Kahneman in a famous scientific paper (Tversky & Kahneman, 1974). The *representativeness heuristic* is close to stereotypical thinking and refers to the tendency to evaluate the likelihood that a phenomenon belongs to a certain category if it resembles the prototypical idea one has of the phenomenon ("*it looks like, therefore it must be*"...). The *availability heuristic* occurs when people estimate the probability or frequency of an event by using what comes to mind as an indicator when they "*assess the frequency of a class or the probability of an event by the ease with which instances or occurrences can be brought to mind*" (Tversky & Kahneman, 1974, p. 1127). For example, the competition for audience ratings between TV channels or newspapers tends to generate sensationalism. By running similar topics over and over again, such as street crime (over, say, white-collar crime), TV channels fill citizens' memories with petty crime stories, thus leading them to consider lawlessness as being "huge", overestimation that can lead to behaviors such as scapegoating, distrust, unnecessary avoidance behavior, survivalist preparation, vigilantism, etc. Fortunately, these consequences can themselves generate positive short-term economic outcomes such as the purchase of alarm systems, cameras, armored doors, weapons, self-defense and meditation courses, relaxation books and apps, anxiolytics, moving services, private school tuitions, etc. Lastly, the *anchoring and adjustment heuristic* relates to relying on a piece of information as a reference point ("anchor"), however accurate it might be, to then adjust their final decision when using more available information. One of the most common examples is the bargaining situation: if one is traveling abroad and ignores local prices at the pawn shop, second-hand electronic store, or traditional market, the first prices given by the salespeople will serve as a reference point. They will tend to be high, thus determining a higher final price than if the "anchor" price was lower. Knowing about cognitive biases and heuristics is usually helpful in minimizing compromised judgments. However, biases are not only cognitive: they often have to do with emotions.

3.1.2.4. *Cognitive Distortions and Defense Mechanisms*

Other biases have gained popularity with the extent of the wellness industry and many psychotherapeutic concepts are now common knowledge such as cognitive distortions, biases that mental health professionals deal with daily. But one thing is to know about their existence, another is to domesticate them through regular practice. Being able to control them in the best way possible helps not to get drawn into pessimistic thinking or envisioning (discounting the positive, maximizing the negative, catastrophizing, overgeneralizing from a sole negative element). It is beneficial to remember that we overestimate our objectivity and that controlling false "realism" can make a difference in very hard situations. Being aware of how you tend to negatively label events, others, or yourself, by noticing specific words or mottos in your inner speeches for example ("*I knew it…*", "*Of course!*", etc.) can help you step back and reboot your approach. Indeed, people and situations are often more complex and ambiguous than we perceive them, and engaging in all-or-nothing thinking rarely has long-term benefits. "Should statements" can also have detrimental effects on mental health. Unfortunately, they are being encouraged nowadays by ideological marionettes engaged in a moral crusade against "procrastination" and "excuses".

On an even deeper level, psychoanalysts have uncovered mental and emotional processes that are called "defense mechanisms". Not all lead to significant perceptual bias (regression, somatization, acting out, passive aggression) but some definitely do. They are often more or less distorted from their original meaning such as denial or projection. For example, the way that people in a psychotic state deny or project is different than in the sentence "*Anthony is denying his addiction*" or "*Sharonda is putting things in my head*". A psychotic male with repressed gay tendencies might believe that *you* are the gay one. A conspiracy theorist will deny evidence that refutes his "*idée fixe*". Some other distorting defense mechanisms are not as famous, such as splitting, idealization, or rationalization. The incapacity to admit ambivalent feelings can lead to "splitting" a person or situation into a black-or-white idealization or devaluation, which makes things appear either perfect or despicable. The APA defines rationalization as a defense "*in which apparently logical reasons are given to justify unacceptable behavior that is motivated by unconscious instinctual impulses*" (APA, 2018). Rationalizations are used by people "*to defend against feelings of guilt, maintain self-respect, and protect oneself from criticism*" (APA, 2018). The unconscious nature of these defense mechanisms makes it hard to identify, analyze, and monitor. Acknowledging and controlling biases are important steps in cleaning up the path to clarity. These mental actions solve one problem: how to avoid analytical pitfalls (negative perspective). But the next question needs to be: how to more actively understand actions and situations (positive perspective)?

3.2. Optimizing Active and Accurate Understanding

"There is nothing more practical than a good theory"

Kurt Lewin

Positively understanding actions and situations requires interpretation frameworks and intellectual tools. From professional experience, I am familiar with pedantry as well as anti-intellectual stances consisting, for example, of overvaluing practice over theory. Anti-intellectualism, which can actually be considered as another bias, possesses solid roots and is partly related to the fact that many people believe their personal experience provides them sufficient mastery to deal with anthropological questions. Interestingly, most people wouldn't even think of rejecting the usefulness of theory in domains such as architecture or military strategy. Often, mocking theory finds its roots in negative school experiences that contribute to developing attitudes of resistance towards learning, sometimes related to self-esteem wounds (feeling idiotic when not understanding, having endured humiliating teachers, etc.). However, people still use "theories" when they think they don't (ideological premises, stereotypes, personal opinions about human nature, etc.). What are the arguments in favor of rejecting behavioral science conceptualizations? *"They might be wrong"*? They could, but they have been through heavy critical filtering processes such as uncharitable academic discussions and pitiless peer-reviewed selection. In that sense, they have more worth than self-righteous *TikTok* rants. *"They can be hard to understand"*? Tough luck. Economics too. Amazingly, many wannabee millionaires overcame their dread of reading and magically found the motivation to pick up a book on "crypto" or plutocrats' habits. Understanding is possible: people from uneducated backgrounds rise to academic positions every day. *"Conceptualizations are disconnected from reality?"* Not always: many theories are built upon practical experience and even life-or-death situations (gang zone ethnography, tradecraft or strategy theory, etc.). And even "armchair theorizing" is not always irrelevant. Understanding human behavior takes time and effort, and change comes with a price.

3.2.1. Knowing Behavioral Determinants for Realistic Agency

Historiography of the human and social sciences reveals that historical periods are usually characterized by some dominant model of behavioral explanation[5]. For example, the importance given to biology, heredity, and race during the 1930s and early 1940s was heavily criticized after the war by anthropologists and social psychologists, among others, who emphasized the role of culture and group dynamics in human behavior. In the fifties, empiricism, functionalism, and statistics were heavily engaged in social science and widely

---

5   Among many examples, see: Backhouse, R. E., & Fontaine, P. (2012). *The history of the social sciences since 1945*. Cambridge University Press.

internationalized. In the late 1960s, sociology was partly influenced by historical materialism and psychoanalysis, which both focused on structural and unconscious forces. In the 1980s, the focus started to shift from social classes and groups to individuals, from non-conscious processes to rational and cognitive ones. Neuropsychology and evolutionary psychology, especially in the 1990s, developed rapidly. To a certain extent, intellectual, and scientific development are autonomous, but they are also grounded in economic and political conditions: socialism, fascism, liberalism, or conservatism did shape the production of behavioral sciences as well as the nature/nurture debate.

Twin and adoption studies have shown that biological determinants (genes, neurotransmitters, hormones, etc.) can influence some personality traits, cognitive test performances, or addictive behaviors (Segal, 2013). But trying to understand the behavior of a person or a social situation by using a biological psychology or biological anthropology model will generally provide feebleminded remarks such as: *"Nathaniel has good grades and mild manners because he has excellent genes"* or *"Gabriella started CrossFit to regulate her high testosterone levels"*. Professionals who want or need to comprehend human behavior (behavioral scientists, judges, etc.) sometimes make the effort to consider as many non-biological determinants as possible. Let's go through a few.

Historical and technological development: to understand contemporary teenage issues with authority and relationships, for example, there is no way around considering the genesis of democracy, globalization, and innovations such as smartphones, video games, and social media.

Nature of economic system: According to historian Eric Hobsbawm: " *For 80 percent of humanity the Middle Ages ended suddenly in the 1950s*" (Hobsbawm, 2020, p. 288). The shift from traditional economies to market economies affected social relations, family dynamics and individual behaviors in many parts of the world.

Type of political regimes: dictatorships, which always make heavy use of secret political police, determine "role distance" (a concept proposed by Canadian sociologist Erving Goffman to designate the degree of commitment or adherence to a social role), degrees of trust between individuals and even perhaps "conscientiousness" (a personality trait defined by the APA as *"the tendency to be organized, responsible, and hardworking"*) (APA, 2018).

Ideology: a widespread ideology can determine behaviors such as praying or business launching.

Culture: culture determines behaviors that can be wrongly considered "natural". Proof that male dominance is not universal is established by the existence of matrilinear ethnic groups such as the Mosuo (China) or the Aka of Central Africa, but also of high gender equality rates in Scandinavia.

Degree of corruption: a high level of corruption can lead large parts of the population to develop attitudes such as fatalism and resentment towards the elite.

States of markets: levels of suicide, well-being, and scapegoating vary when economies go through booms or crises (Bursztyn et al., 2022).

Availability of basic goods: accessibility can affect levels of civility in the supermarket.

Sales: humans have created societies where people will tramp others to death during "Black Friday" type events to maximize chances to purchase big-screen TVs at a good price (Crockett Z., 2019).

Extent and quality of public services: in his book, *Punishing the Poor: The Neoliberal Government of Social Insecurity*, Loïc Wacquant shows, among many other harmful policies and dynamics, how they can determine deviance and incarceration levels (Wacquant, 2009). Other works have studied their impact on fertility rates (d'Addio & d'Ercole, 2005): precarious social services can dissuade couples from having a child, consequences that can lead to demographic problems.

Socioeconomic inequalities: The more socioeconomic inequality, the more health and social problems: mental illnesses, homicides, imprisonment rates, life expectancy, etc. (see Figure 1).

Degree of civil liberties: the development of civil liberties can determine the level of "informalization", a concept that refers to the progressive easing up of social conventions or formal rules leading to more relaxed social relations, even among people from different statuses (Wouters, 2007). A head of state being bear-hugged and lifted off the ground by a playful pizzeria owner was a unique phenomenon in the history of mankind.

Ethnic relations: their deterioration, by an economic crisis and a subsequent election, for example, can most certainly have an impact on the scapegoats' supposedly personality traits, such as "agreeableness". Sociolinguists could probably demonstrate that the tone in which underpaid staff will take fast-food orders can depend on political circumstances.

Unemployment rate: high ones can statistically contribute to addictive behaviors and helplessness (Arena et al., 2023).

Amount of economic and cultural capital within the social space of a nation: the sociologist Pierre Bourdieu established that behaviors such as sports practices, music listening, drink preferences, or voting were structurally determined by the amount of economic and cultural capital of individuals, not enchanted individual inclination (Bourdieu, 1985).

Location within the social space of a specific field: Pierre Bourdieu also established that behavioral strategies can be shaped by one's position in a field (a system of objective relations between positions in the artistic, military, or corporate world, etc.). For example, a dominant CEO can play it cool and act modestly by just wearing a T-shirt because he doesn't have anything to prove, while a "young wolf" might, on the contrary, behave more aggressively and overdress. Elite special forces operators will tend to act very nonchalantly and be more hairy than less prestigious military personnel who are condemned to buzz cuts and stiff postures.

Corporate identity: working for two decades for, say, *Google, JPMorgan Chase*, or *Tony & Guy* will shape employees' dressing styles, eating habits, and partner choices differently.

Workplace environment: management policy and mode will determine the quality of relationships, sleep, motivation, loyalty, etc.[6]

Primary socialization and family upbringing: Initial living conditions and socialization processes have a deep impact on future behaviors and mental health (Scheid & Brown, 2012). But these well-known relations are not unilateral: a working-class family can provide a stable and favorable emotional environment to a child who can develop as a fulfilled adult while a dysfunctional upper-middle-class family ridden by secrets, incest, or rivalry can lead an otherwise privileged sibling to prison, a psychiatric ward, or a graveyard.

Secondary socialization: the socialization that takes place in high school, the neighborhood, at work, or on social media has a lasting but not necessarily definitive impact (peer

---

6   Many studies on the psychosocial effects of leadership styles have followed the pioneering work of Kurt Lewin (Lewin et al., 1939). For example, see: Das & Pattanayak (2023).

pressure, embodied norms, and attitudes, etc.), on musical tastes, dressing style, political orientation, sexual partner preference, philosophical ideas, career choice, leisure activities, quality and quantity of physical activity, life "hygiene", etc. To grasp the influence of secondary socialization, one can just imagine the possible differences between two elderly monozygotic twins separated from birth and raised in two different countries and two different social classes.

Habitus: socialization forms "*a system of lasting dispositions which integrate past and present perceptions, appreciations, and actions, and also facilitate the achievement of an open-ended array of diversified tasks*" (Cohen, 2006, p. 259). Pierre Bourdieu stressed the importance of understanding "practice" by considering the interplay between habitus (a sort of social personality) and the field of relations individuals are engaged in. Habitus can be attached to a social class, a subculture, or a profession, and generate similar actions and reactions in people who have been socialized in a close manner. It can be perceptible, for example, in a body posture, making it sometimes possible for two strangers possessing a similar habitus to "recognize" each other in a group or crowd (waiting room, collective audition, subway wagon, etc.), immediately get along, or "instinctively" feel antipathy.

Sexual orientation: sexual orientation can occasionally determine practices and proprieties other than sexual (political behavior, aesthetic choices, form of gait, sociolinguistic characteristics, etc.).

Personality dimensions: some specialists work with only five, some others with dozens. Five seems too limited but serious works support this starting point model. The APA presents the "Big Five personality model" as: *"a model of the primary dimensions of individual differences in personality. The dimensions are usually labeled extraversion, neuroticism, agreeableness, conscientiousness, and openness to experience"* (APA, 2018). Neuroticism, according to the APA, is *"characterized by a chronic level of emotional instability and proneness to psychological distress."* (APA, 2018). Maybe not be the most precise concept ever but it is widely in use.

Personality disorder: about 8% of the world population is estimated to have a personality disorder (Winsper et al., 2020). That's not bad, almost one in ten people. Of course, a higher percentage of people have a normal symptom here and there without being psychiatrically eligible. According to the APA: a personality disorder is *"any in a group of disorders involving pervasive patterns of perceiving, relating to, and thinking about the environment and the self that interfere with long-term functioning of the individual and are not limited to isolated episodes"* (APA, 2023).

Contingency: Often, observers tend to forget that situations can happen fortuitously. However, political analysts, for example, can be struck in their theoretical model (Domino theory, etc.) and apply it by force, while non-experts can fall victim to common sense magical thinking and believe *"everything happens for a reason"*.

3.2.2. Mastering Critical Thinking Tools

Once a few precautions are taken, and a little knowledge is accumulated, one can apply heuristics as well as critical thinking tools when the amount of information required to think produces cognitive overload. Critical thinking involves dispositions that we mentioned earlier: it requires the will to understand accurately, some curiosity, open-mindedness, and metacognitive reflection. This is not the place to go into details concerning specific problem-solving and decision-making methods. It is nevertheless timely to discuss the topics of data evaluation, analysis, and interpretation.

Data evaluation essentially entails estimating the quality, credibility, and significance of the information. Is the observation tool performant (lens, thermometer, mind, etc.)? Is the information accurate enough to use for analysis and interpretation, or is it too vague? Is it credible? Who's speaking? An independent mind like Noam Chomsky or a PR mouthpiece for Big Pharma? Is the information obtained pertinent for the issue to be solved?

Analysis often starts by clarifying information, ideas, and assumptions, by simplifying and organizing. What's the problem? Is there only one? Could there be several, agglutinated together? Do we deal with all the elements of the problem at once? Is the problem well framed (*"That's because you're a loser"*)? Or free from gross assumptions (*"Darling, Paris is just going to be magical…"*)? Some questions might appear fundamental, but do they really have an answer ("*These commuters look so depressed: couldn't we have built more ludicrous societies?*", "*Gee, couldn't we wear jollier colors like the Indians?*", "*Why is this happening to me?!*")? Is it urgent to answer this question now ("*How much is it going to cost me to get this stain removed from my shirt?*")? Is the question sterile? (*Mike!* [a 2-year-old], *why did you throw your spoon?!*", "*Can't we all just get along?*").

Interpretation is about how you make sense of the information. For that, you need frameworks, possibly ones that don't rely on vague and general "laws" but on multiple viewpoints and details, on historical and contextual knowledge. Interpretation often deals with trying to answer the question "why?". "*Why did this person do this?*", "*Why did this happen?*" Many people or professionals need to handle these questions (parents, high school headmasters, judges, sociologists, journalists, foreign affairs analysts, etc.). But not all actors being asked the question "why?" are equally trustworthy: an accomplice might trivialize the infraction motives, a lawyer could use rhetorical techniques to blame the other party more convincingly, etc. Other professionals are only paid to give facts, without being asked for an interpretation. Their job stops at the descriptive level, to answer the question "How?" Countless individuals don't even care about motives and causes: parents might give up on the idea of determining "*who started this?*", or a not-so-curious person might say, like in a Hollywoodian happy-end: "*all that matters is that the problem is over now*".

As we wrote earlier to encourage readers, observing and understanding can provide the by-product of satisfaction, not only during the process but also in the outcome. Yet, accessing pleasure in the act of thinking requires method and training, just as an athlete executing a difficult and successful coordination of movements. The now famous concept of "flow" elaborated by psychologist Mihály Csíkszentmihályi, which is not often associated with the activity of thinking, designates a state that involves some difficulty and acquired competence, *"when one's skills are fully utilized yet equal to the demands of the task[7]"*. Without the skills, the "demand" can't be met, and the "task" is much less likely to be enjoyable. Skill is thus a key element to enjoyment, even though its acquisition can be harsh.

---

7   Here is the full definition: *"a state of optimal experience arising from intense involvement in an activity that is enjoyable, such as playing a sport, performing a musical passage, or writing a creative piece. Flow arises when one's skills are fully utilized yet equal to the demands of the task, intrinsic motivation is at a peak, one loses self-consciousness and temporal awareness, and one has a sense of total control, effortlessness, and complete concentration on the immediate situation (the here and now)"* (APA, 2018).

CHAPTER 4
Step 3: Adaptation

❧

Adaptation, whether understood as a process or outcome, is a concept used in different disciplines. In biology, there are no values attached to the phenomenon. Even though some scholars still want to draw moral conclusions from the observation of nature, biological adaptation only refers to *"all internal and external correlations (organism-milieu relations) that allow an organism to live in a certain manner in a given habitat, and to contribute to the perpetuation of the species to which it belongs"* (Boquet, 2002, as cited in Simonet, 2010, p.6). But in the field of psychology, things get more complicated. While the definitions of adaptation in biological psychology are close to the biological one above (*"adjustment of a sense organ to the intensity or quality of stimulation"* (APA, 2018) or *"reduced responsiveness in a sensory receptor or sensory system caused by prolonged or repeated stimulation"*(APA, 2018), the characterization of adaptation in clinical psychology can appear problematic. Let's take a look at one proposed by the APA :

"adjustments to the demands, restrictions, and mores of society, including the ability to live and work harmoniously with others

and to engage in satisfying social interactions and relationships." (APA, 2018).

Obviously, there appears to be something "good" about adaptation in this definition ("harmony", "satisfaction", etc.). According to this proposition, one could have been doing quite well in occupied France. But today, an Anarchist living in the United States, or a capitalist residing in Cuba would probably have comments on this definition. Indeed, adaptation is closely related to mental health in psychology. The APA suggests another meaning:

-*"modification to suit different or changing circumstances. In this sense, the term often refers to behavior that enables an individual to adjust to the environment effectively and function optimally in various domains, such as coping with daily stressors."* (APA, 2018).

This definition seems valid because quite adequate and objective. However, from a historical, sociological, or anthropological stance, notions such as "effective adjustment" or "optimal functioning" appear slightly normative and culturally biased. Indeed, they involve the notion of performance and excellence. It is also partly affected by the bias of functionalism which *"views mental life and behavior in terms of active adaptation to environmental challenges and opportunities"* (APA, 2018). Other approaches in psychology such as phenomenology or existential psychology that *"emphasizes the subjective meaning of human experience"* (APA, 2018) do not consider a motherly or fatherly act of caressing a child's hair as "optimal parental functioning". There is also something awkward in the Western psychologized culture of perceiving one's acts through a utilitarian lens or labeling one's daily tasks or companions as possible "stressors" requiring the application of "coping skills" to sustain "well-being" and "mental health"[8].

Similar to "effective adjustment", "adaptive behavior" is defined by the APA as :

-*"the level of everyday performance of tasks that is required for a person to fulfill typical roles in society, including maintaining independence and meeting cultural expectations regarding personal and social responsibility."* (APA, 2023).

This is interesting. To our knowledge, *"independence"* and *"responsibility"* are not scientific concepts. They are values. And thankfully, not everybody is *"meeting cultural expectations"*. The definition of *"adaptive behavior"* gets better:

"Specific categories in which adaptive behavior is usually assessed include self-help, mobility, health care, communication, domestic skills, consumer skills, community use, practical academic skills, and vocational skills." (APA, 2023).

---

8   For an interesting discussion of psychologism in the West, see: Rose, N. (2012). *Inventing Ourselves: Psychology, power, and personhood.* Cambridge University Press.

Assessing domestic, consumer, and vocational skills sounds more like what a social worker would do during a "home visit" than what a Beverly Hills therapist would discuss in her office with… Beverly.

There is little doubt that the concept of adaptation in psychology is "value-laden" and contains a conformist bias. But the APA *Dictionary of Psychology* possesses a more neutral entry for "*adjustment process*", defined as:

> "*any means through which human beings modify attitudes and behaviors in response to environmental demands. Such attempts to maintain a balance between needs and the circumstances that influence the satisfaction of those needs are influenced by numerous factors that vary widely across situations and individuals and are the subject of much research.*" (APA, 2018).

Some APA definitions might be disputable, but they are nevertheless the product of decades of research by scientists who devoted their lives to the idea that it is possible to approach objectivity by using rational means.

The *Fulatune* method doesn't advocate "*meeting cultural expectations*" *per se* or adapting to mainstream or alternative social orders. Besides, adaptation is understood here from the standpoint of an individual, a group, or an institution facing alternatives. This chapter will also focus on behavioral adaptations rather than physiological ones.

4.1. Why Adapt? After All...

Consequences of inadaptation can be (very) uncomfortable but tolerable. If, for philosophical reasons, you are willing to pay the price of conscious inadaptation (job precarity, chronic debt, repetitive legal issues, conflictual relationships, stress-related diseases, etc.), it can be a justifiable choice. And if the rebellious attitude leads to passing down some memorable cultural production to humanity (song, book, theorem, painting, etc.), that's even better. Otherwise, you might only be remembered as a grumpy neighbor.

Voluntary inadaptation to facts (not requiring our existence to be, independent from our perception or will) will not be categorized as denial (since refusal to adapt is in this case intentional), but it could lead to the same outcome: failure. Idealistic bias, self-image distortion, and moral principles are often implied in this problem: *"You can (always) make it if you try!"*, *"I'm tougher than him/her/em!"*, *"This is unacceptable!"*, etc. Adaptation often requires some flexibility and compromise. But if the compromise feels like a compromission, you don't have to go through your project. Our approach doesn't endorse the idea that one should let go of moral standards or a sense of honor to achieve a goal. It is not uncommon to hear people advise others to let go of their pride (*"What do you care!?"*). However, these everyday counselors are missing out on the fact that social honor is closely related to mental health. They even might be the first ones to cling to conspicuous consumption commodities such as sacrosanct European handbags.

Generally, real inadaptation or feelings of inadequacy aren't intended, but undergone: *"Does my rococo villa really epitomize my core self after all?"*, *"Will this audience recognize my expertise?"*, *"Why am I systematically ending up with these types of blokes?"*, *"After 15 years in this company, I still find these double standards revolting!"*, *"Could I actually stay clean for the next half century?"*, *"Will I be able to live with myself if I became a snitch"*, *"Should I realistically undertake accounting retraining, or rather, as my guru suggested, follow my dream of becoming a professional poet ?"* Unresolved discordance can lead to chronic anxiety that could be misdiagnosed as a hereditary neuroticism predisposition and inaugurate a lifetime under Benzodiazepine. In its lighter forms, it can prompt feelings of lasting discomfort such as the "imposter syndrome". If unresolved, feelings of ineptitude can generate states close to "learned helplessness": *"a phenomenon in which repeated exposure to uncontrollable stressors results in individuals failing to use any control options that may later become available. Essentially, individuals are said to learn that they lack behavioral control over environmental events, which, in turn, undermines the motivation to make changes or attempt to alter situations."* (APA, 2018). Learning adaptation skills can thus be vital.

4.2. Adapt to What?

Adaptation can be a matter of physical or symbolic survival: maladaptive skills can destroy your body or reputation[9]. For example, an uncontrolled pride chin movement in jail might get you iced-picked the next day. Or naïvely believing you could let your guard down, get loose, and tipsy at the team-building office party could ruin your candidacy for some appealing manager position. Certain people are so committed to their social role that they don't need to adapt; they already are, like a fish in water. These individuals are not exclusively found in remote traditional cultures (in which challenging one's social assignment can be less frequent than in postmodern ones). People evolving in futuristic settings can also demonstrate a high degree of cultural conformism (Silicon Valley coffee shops, K-Pop concerts, etc.). Primary and/or secondary socialization can engender an almost perfect match between role and soul. Yet, many people are in a discordant situation, one in which their habitus is not congruent with the field they must or want to engage in (a North African doctor having to make ends meet as a nurse in France, a young woman from *Vila Cruzeiro* favela working for *Elite Model Management*, a novelist from a working-class background dinning at the *Nobel Banquet*, etc.).

---

9   The APA dictionary of psychology defines maladaptation as: "*a condition in which biological traits or behavior patterns are detrimental, counterproductive, or otherwise interfere with optimal functioning in various domains, such as successful interaction with the environment and effectual coping with the challenges and stresses of daily life.*" (APA, 2018)

Billions of people find themselves in circumstances where their mindset, desires, or skills don't closely correspond to the environment's requisites. In those cases, people use different strategies: they can overemphasize incompetence, in the hope some guardian angel will become their mentor, they can act "as if" they possessed the skill and then bluff their way through, or parallelly engage in a skill acquisition process. At some point, other individuals might judge the efforts required to adjust aren't worth it and decide to leave the game (dropping the *Iditarod Trail Invitational*, refusing to take orders from a deviously racist subchief at a luncheonette, etc.). If they can: many people don't have an immediate choice, like so many *maquiladora* workers.

Adapting often means adjusting to adverse situations. Many people have a hard time with that process. And the fact that some cannot cope doesn't make them "losers", as many simplistic and binary worldviews suggest. The ones who couldn't take extremely enduring situations such as the 1929 economic crisis, torture, or addiction in sepulchral towns struck by unemployment deserve respect. Besides, no one knows how they will react under truly harsh circumstances: wartime biographies show that peacetime bragging machos can crack under pressure while more modest women, like Noor Inayat Khan (Basu, 2006) or Germaine Tillion (Tillion & Lacouture, 2000), will endure the toughest treatments.

Life can be tough almost anywhere, even in globally rich cities such as London, Paris, or Berlin, all characterized by huge socioeconomic inequalities, precarious work conditions, and petty crime. Not to mention the gloomy winters, underground, and landscapes. Sure enough, life is even worse in Lagos, Manilla, or Caracas. But migrants from those megapolises wouldn't necessarily feel living and raising children in West Bronx, Saint-Denis or Molenbeek is paradise either. Not to mention that trying to "survive" as a precarious lower middle-class freelance in Manhattan, with the outrageous prices, rents, competition, contract uncertainties, and lifestyle social pressure, can be challenging too. Even more secure jobs can be very demanding: being a civil servant such as a nurse or a social worker but working for decades with drug addicts or deprived groups in poor areas is definitely taxing. Even devoted and seemingly well-off managers can commit suicide (Nossiter, 2019).

Adverse situations do come in different degrees:

-Highly adverse situations can be, for example, trying to pass selection processes at Japanese intelligence agencies[10], top American consulting firms, or the French École normale supérieure. It can be acculturing to a prison term for a not so "prestigious" felony like insider trading crime, to a new country as an asylum seeker, to an abusive father, to a working-class school as an effeminate boy.

-Intermediate adverse situations might be going through a series of job interviews at Google for a manager's position, becoming a young Wall Street trader, getting as athletic as

---

10 Never heard about them? That's how good they are.

the other CrossFit club members, or dealing with a sarcastic supervisor daily.

-Low adverse situations can be related to bearing unpleasant work atmospheres, long, depressing, and unreliable commuting, obligatory mundane gatherings, a dull marriage, recurring neighboring dog barks while working from home, etc. Sometimes memorizing lessons, applying cognitive restructuring, or "letting go" is not enough. So how does one optimally adapt?

4.3. How to Adapt

Effective adaptation, in its conscious form, starts with observing (step one) and understanding (step 2) as accurately as possible a behavior or situation. Concerning a behavior, understanding its possible determinants, objectives, and consequences in a dynamic context will help determine a decision concerning a course of (re)action(s). You might not have sketched out a plan. If the behavior pops out of nowhere, like street harassment, domestic violence, or terrorism, you might want to remember what your most important objective is (survive, save face, get to the destination on time, protect companion or children) and determine a few options (fight, flight, freeze, ignore, persuade, etc.). If you had to some extent anticipated the behavior or event, you would have saved some decision-making time and reduced the risk of emotions getting in the way too much. For example, by anticipating that the clerk was probably going to be sardonically unhelpful to you when confused by awkward signage logic at Charles de Gaulle airport, you could have stayed cool and gotten what you wanted by being "broken record" assertive. Concerning a situation, having appropriately analyzed and understood its stakes and implicit demands can contribute to adequate adaptation, which usually occurs as a fluid unfolding of the sequence: minimal ambiguity, misunderstanding, hesitation, or awkwardness. Adapting accordingly to social situations is not that usual or easy. Many situations go south daily: disregarding one's tone of voice or posture with an authority figure, cracking a dubious joke on the first meeting with possible stepparents, believing people generally absolve dress-code deviance, being pedant to arouse admiration, trying out a flirtatiousness tactic with the magistrate, etc.

Theoretical and practical knowledge is crucial to adaptation. In some of the examples above, learning relates to new norms, behaviors, coping skills, problem-solving skills, etc. Coping skills are essential during energy-taxing adjustment processes: uncertainty can generate anxiety and decision-making is proven to deplete willpower and cause fatigue (Baumeister & Tierney, 2011). Therefore, adaptation calls for endurance and motivation, especially when some adaptation steps fail. Regular feedback and rewards can help carry on the development and recast the adjustment dynamic. Acclimation also requires resources in the form of time, technical and emotional support, garments, money, etc. It can be done without much thinking, but having a plan is most certainly beneficial. Even a vague objective will operate as a signpost to avoid some obstacles, determine small steps, and maintain an itinerary (long periods can come with off-course deviations, be associated with distractions, and give rise to new goals). For example, a student might, out of financial necessity, see his side gig transform itself into a full-time job. He could also, through socialization, turn into a juiced party animal. Maternity and social pressure can lead a young woman to progressively abandon her career dreams to raise her children full-time. An ex-convict can forget about staying legit and relapse into the deviant activities that got him into trouble in the first place. Remaining on the course of the adaptation path involves incentives that are occasionally worth the discomfort of giving up old behaviors.

Reaching adaptation goals is facilitated today by the huge amount of mainly American science surrounding "goal setting" and "motivation". One of the most important and complex steps in reaching goals is outlining a plan (and, of course, implementing it). Plan development, especially for complex social situations, implies considering many factors (resources, obstacles, alternatives, virtual outcomes, etc.). Figuring out effective solutions, which are often adaptive coping responses, is generally a challenging and draining exercise. This is why assistance from experts can be necessary. At this stage, different forms of resistance can occur: contempt for depending on external assistance, for "theory", for some aspects of the new environment's values, etc. It is not always possible to overcome these obstacles. But it helps to remember, though, that external and specialized assistance represents a considerable gain of time and can bolster prevention against foolish attitudes such as barking up the wrong tree. For those who dislike "theory", it is crucial to restate that theory is often inductively built upon practice: just think how useful the "Moscow rules" (a list of tradecraft precautions acquired the hard way) were to generations of case officers. Resistance also comes from clinging to old values that the present environment has made futile or prejudicial: picture all the burned-out people trying to quit their now meaningless jobs or vain social media activity. Because resistance can linger on while executing the plan, it can be wise to regularly refer to some kind of pre-established cost-benefit matrix to stay determined.

The stage of practical plan execution is of course crucial. Some people will be better at it, while others will be more skilled at elaborating solutions on paper. Plan enactment is often stressful and difficult (rehearsing interviews, controlling live performances, repeating High-Intensity Interval Training, etc.). Recovery periods are therefore fundamental to replenish mental and physical resources during this stage. Recovery is rarely a waste of time as it often can feel. Micro-adaptations occur during this period in the sense of *"reduced responsiveness in a sensory receptor or sensory system caused by prolonged or repeated stimulation"* (APA, 2018): less anxiety, less pain, less oxygen debt. Monitoring this process allows us to make readjustments and help remain diligent by acknowledging quantitative or qualitative progress. Eventually, the adaptation *process* will lead to an adaptation *state*: being ready to effectively respond to the new environmental demands.

Figure 6. *The Observe, Understand, Adapt (OUA) process*

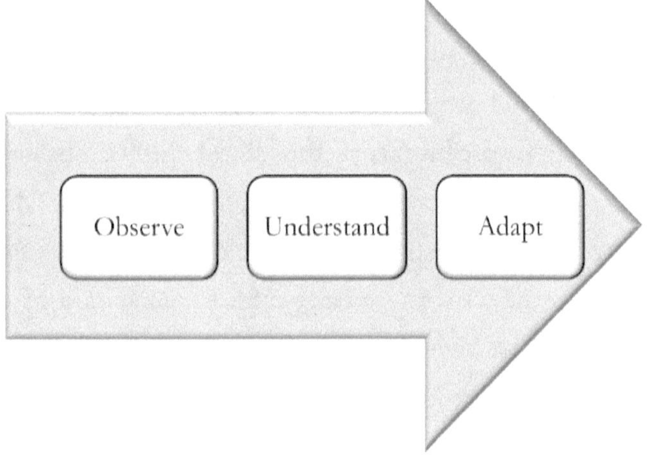

PART II
Principles, Steps & Programs

The first part introduced the biopsychosocial foundations and the three main stages of our approach. This second part is more practical as it specifies concretely how the acts of preparing, observing, and interpreting can be applied rationally and efficiently. Chapter 5 condenses into principles important points discussed in part one and transparently shares the mechanisms that make the *Fulatune* method operational. It then enumerates steps that can help coherently organize actions leading to fruitful adaptation. Chapter 6 then presents several areas and topics to which the method can be applied.

CHAPTER 5
Principles, Mechanisms, and Steps

❧

The *Fulatune* method aims at optimizing adaptation processes by observing specific principles and steps. It intends to reinforce awareness and hardiness. Firstly, three cornerstones that encapsulate essential recommendations are presented. Secondly, essential mechanisms involved in the adaptation processes are specified. Thirdly, a detailed procedure of progressive steps is proposed as a guideline.

5.1. Three Principles and Rational Mechanisms

Before considering the steps in a detailed manner, it is preferable to understand how they ensue from core principles and operate by means of real and efficient change processes.

5.1.1. Three Principles

Principle 1. Building the Best Biopsychosocial Foundations Possible
This principle is based upon a materialistic position: engaging in cognitive restructuring will be less effective if your body is craving for nutriments or sleep and if your willpower is

not supported by social networks and resources (emotional, technical, emotional support). Even if you are on your own and broke, you should still try to fulfill as many physiological needs as possible. For example, *Special Air Service* (SAS) operators are taught not to defiantly refuse food and water during captivity and interrogations (Clay, 2003). Besides, waiting until hard times crop up to start practicing cognitive restructuring and relaxation techniques is not a good idea: the sooner the better. As a prevention act, you already want to have somewhat mastered these cognitive and behavioral skills.

Principle 2. Following the Observe, Understand, Adapt (OUA) Sequence

This principle applies to cases when you have a little time in front of you; not when emergencies brutally occur and engage you in intuitive decision-making processes. This principle is not obvious. Indeed, many people skip the observation phase and think they already understood, just like when someone finishes your sentence for you, and gets it wrong. Conversely, *you* might be the one skipping the observation phase. For self-esteem reasons, we sometimes tend to overestimate our abilities. Lack of worldliness is closely associated with naïveté, which can lead to partial or total unawareness of situational elements. This form of innocence can prompt problems: a romantic walkabout in Naples ending up in Camorra-controlled territory, your excellent mood making you overlook the fact that your boss was observing you letting it all hang out near the coffee machine. Being observant helps detect discreet environmental details and patterns: something out of place, an overdressed person, colleagues acting unusually disciplined, or three people moving synchronically in a crowd. Unfortunately, there is no real shortcut to becoming more intuitive and worldly-wise. Pride very frequently comes in the way of learning and the "hard way" remains the unrivaled pedagogical method. You might ask: "*But doesn't following the OUA sequence generate a loss in spontaneity?*" It sure does since anticipation is a key element of it. But this handbook isn't about unrehearsed club strutting or enhancing creative processes for artists anyway. There is a time for everything and, as a matter of fact, great artists know that improvisation often takes long initiation and not-so-spontaneous training. Lastly, preparation and spontaneity are not always antithetical: good anticipation can make you react more rapidly when it's on.

Principle 3. Preparing, Practicing, and Recovering Regularly
Good observation skills habitually depend on being prepared and knowing what to look for (having a framework). Anticipation takes a little time, but the benefits can be great. For example, by expecting an event, you can reduce the emotional response it triggers and remain confident by having a plan B in mind. Mental anticipation can be supplemented by behavioral preparation. The job interview example being overused, let's say you sense tension is building up in your

team and that some kind of catharsis will probably burst in the next few days or weeks if nothing is done. Depending on your role in the team (subordinate, manager), you might want to set some general goals, such as avoiding being the scapegoat or preparing conditions for constructive talk. To desensitize yourself a bit from the anxiety this anticipation might create, you can visualize possible scenarios concerning the location of the crisis, the person through which it will likely actualize itself (hot-tempered Butch perhaps?), the potential pretexts masquerading as the real problem (the staples disappeared "again"), etc. On a behavioral level, you can start writing out how you could best react to innuendo or straight-up blaming. You can also build "if, then" scenarios so you don't get caught off guard. If you believe a big storm is inevitably coming, you can start saving your energy and improving your health to face it with strength. If you feel you might need to be assertive, you could practice a few non-escalading punchlines in front of the mirror, as a good actor would do for a great role. Ridiculous? Perhaps. But one cool and supposedly unpremeditated retort, and you can go down in (local) history. Considering the widespread lack of skills in terms of crisis management, the odds are high that the predicament will persist for a while. So, it's a good idea to recover regularly from the stress, but without over-indulging with legal or illegal anxiolytics. There will be no shame, though, in accepting your doctor's prescription if the episode turns into a long-term nightmare. Chronic lack of sleep will get to anybody.

Figure 7. *Three* Fulatune *principles*

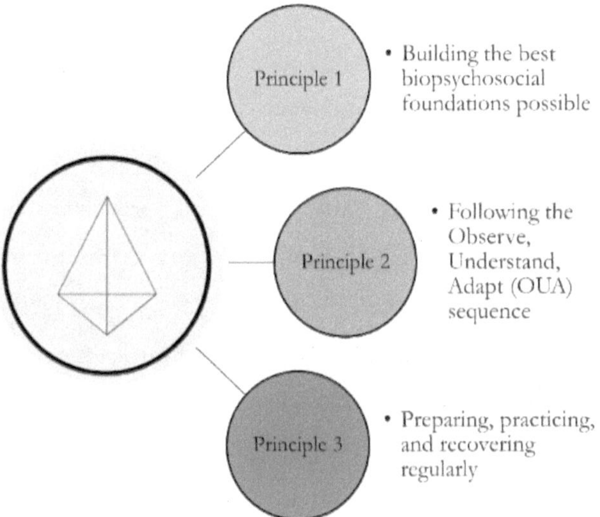

5.1.2. Rational Mechanisms

How are these principles harnessed? The *Fulatune* approach doesn't resort to suggestion or incantation-type processes. It operates through plain preparation (anticipation, planning), cognitive, emotional, and practical learning involving *"consciously or nonconsciously attending to relevant aspects of incoming information, mentally organizing the information into a coherent cognitive representation, and integrating it with relevant existing knowledge activated from long-term memory"* (APA, 2018). It also relies on basic repetition, conditioning, and habit formation.

Repetition is boring and potentially debilitating. But there is just no way around it yet. Mimicry is also a powerful change mechanism. Not a very popular one indeed given the weight of certain values such as "originality" and "uniqueness". But remember these qualities often develop from commonness: great thinkers, architects, or athletes all had to assimilate and replicate actions that were not theirs before they became "original". The French author Édouard Louis, who went through inconceivable trials and tribulations, very honestly admitted using rational mimicry in his impressive transformational process (Louis, 2021). The facilitating processes of progress monitoring and reward self-attribution are also inherent to the *Fulatune* method.

5.2. 16 Steps

Step 1. Setting up a thinking space

A lot of people had a hard time with school. Many apprehend any situation reminding them of this partly force-feeding ordeal. One of the messages contained in this book is that thinking can be not only satisfying *per se* but also rewarding if done methodically and constructively. Falling for botched reasoning is widespread (automatic mottos, binary equations, plain images, self-righteous verdicts, etc.). So much pure action. So many hasty decisions made while fidgeting with our smartphones in public transportation or cars. It is a miracle the world is not doing worse than it already is. Practical sense undoubtedly holds a certain wisdom, but it will never beat the right combination of experienced intuition and logical analysis. Setting up a thinking space and regularly taking time for calm reflection is highly recommended. It helps to have a specific place, a containing setting, so the brain can associate the problem-solving activity with a certain area (preferably not the bedroom). Circumscribing this rational behavior can also help the ego set boundaries and limit intrusive emotions or cognitions during other periods of the day (or night…).

Step 2. Working on your "problem orientation"

If you tend to be misanthropic or pessimistic, and by chance admit it, it is advisable to start working on your problem orientation. On the contrary, if you are inclined to overlook negatives and recite optimistic mantras every morning, it is judicious that you work on your problem-orientation too. Yes, there are objective reasons to feel bad. Coping with problems is unpleasant, time-consuming, and tiring. Nevertheless, negative emotions, if analyzed accurately, can highlight the origins of some problems, and thus contribute to the elaboration of solution plans. Everybody avoids solving certain problems now and then by procrastinating, binging, denying, regressing, wishful thinking, blaming, etc. Even though wait-and-see tactics are far from being foolish at times, problems do tend to persist and worsen if left untreated. Conversely, being over-optimistic can lead to unwise perseverance, whether the attitude is determined by an upbeat ideology or simple ingenuousness. "Positive problem orientation", as understood in Social Problem-Solving therapy, is not beamish: it entails the idea that successful problem-solving involves time and effort.

Step 3. Consolidating biopsychosocial foundations

To possess the stamina and endurance for a possibly taxing and long adaptation process, the *Fulatune* method includes a period of biopsychosocial conditions building. Too many ideological victims run into projects while already physiologically drained from preparation, over-relying on "psyching up" with Coué style methods and overestimating the power of "believing in oneself" while neglecting instrumental and social support networks. Positive psychology techniques can sometimes mitigate the negative effects of physiological and social deprivation. Not everybody benefits from all those resources. In case of shortages, it is always best to stack up as much as possible.

Step 4. Depicting the situation

Before defining the problem, it is important to describe the situation as objectively as possible. The *Fulatune* method is not a perspectivist approach according to which "*the world forms a complex of interacting interpretive processes in which every entity views every entity and event from an orientation peculiar to itself*" (Merriam-Webster, n.d.) While it, of course, recognizes the weight of standpoints and subjectivity in human affairs, it also considers that, because certain elements of reality are independent of our will and consciousness, some phenomena can be perceived the same way by many different people (*"you can't fool all the people all the time"*). To approach a situation objectively is generally difficult since it usually implies *"breaking bones in one's head"*, to paraphrase Jean-Paul Sartre (de Beauvoir & Sartre, 2017), and adopting the point of view of others we may dislike, only reluctantly identifying with them (like profilers or case officers need to do for example). Yuri Modin, Kim Philby's handler at some point, underlined that one of Philby's unique qualities as a master spy was the ability to dispassionately picture a situation from all the actors' viewpoints (Modin, 1994). Reconstructing the positional "space of viewpoints" is actually a methodological moment in sociological field analysis. Of course, few people can technically engage in such global grasping. The main idea is nevertheless to rise above one's narrow perception. Describing a situation can seem obvious, but it is not. Often, people leap this part and have already problematized a situation without even knowing it, leading to false assumptions or badly formulated problems (*"He would never dare"*, *"I lost* [misplaced] *my phone!"*, *"This crying baby is testing me!"*, etc.). Sticking to the facts also helps to cool down and keep it simple: if you are joining a new work environment, the situation is one of employment, and in a hiring situation, the newcomer is expected to be operational rather quickly and able to fit in as well as possible. It is normal to be under some pressure.

Step 5. Defining the problem

Problems emerge from factual situations; they don't appear out of the blue, they are constructed by actors. Perceptions of "unfairly poky" advancement might not be shared by your colleagues or the boss (which doesn't mean they are wrong for all that). Uncertainty is often unnerving, but the problem definition phase is not yet about identifying causes. At this stage, the question is not about discovering if the perceived or real sluggish pace of advancement is determined by personal flaws, a grandiosity symptom, a plot, romantic partner insinuations, the economy, structural racism, affirmative action policies, office politics, China's rise, etc. It is more about building a logical statement to formulate an exploitable question. Institutions specializing in problem-solving and academic research train their members to become efficient at defining problems by trouble-shooting assertions and reformulating problems. For example, exclusively framing violent behavior against a minority group member as a "hate crime" tends to reduce the social problem of systemic discrimination to a psychological motive, a negative emotion, and circularly condemns policies to ineffective problem-solving, law enforcement staff to burn-out, and victims to continual injustice. Very hard to get rid of those bad concepts once they are institutionalized. If one is hired in an unknown work setting, the problem of "proving oneself" is objectively at stake. After all, expectations are legitimate: the first screening test is passed, and people want to know if the interview content was all talk or not. But defining the problem as *"needing to kill it"* or *"it's all about survival"* might add unnecessary stress to the adaptation process. Characterizing in a more balanced way, in terms of *"satisfactory efficiency and integration during the first weeks"*, allows room for probable errors, limited self-blaming, and reasonable coolness. This type of reframing does not celebrate mediocrity; showing excellence can wait until basic new skills are acquired.

Step 6. Raising preliminary goals and questions

Once you've defined a problem under a particular perspective, you can set a general goal and formulate a question relating to its attainment. Since you lack data concerning the environment at this stage, it can be premature to be specific. A general course of action is enough and can always be refined at a later stage. Before your first day, you can simply aim at learning and performing efficiently while socializing agreeably. If you immediately aim at impressing hierarchy, you might unnecessarily pressure yourself and come across as a threat in the eyes of your colleagues by bringing to light what they haven't been doing as well as they could have, prompting the boss to consider them less favorably and to raise his standards without swelling the salaries. It might be best to think twice and start with something like *"How to become relatively efficient and fit in as well as possible without becoming a flunky or a pariah?"*.

Step 7. Observing and collecting data

At this stage, you should be reasonably optimistic, bolstered, and fit. You also know more clearly what problem you're trying to solve, what you want or need, and what to look for in the environment (primary framework). You are now well prepared for observation. Understanding the whole system you integrate is important so you have the full picture in mind when you look at the institutional elements. It also reduces bewilderment and vague anxiety to know where the important sectors are (human resource and CEO office, trade union cubbyhole, bathroom, etc.) and understand the organizational chart (as well as the informal one). People will probably try to pull you very quickly into their clans and intrigues while trying to frame your worldview according to their interests. During this phase, it is advisable to put on a Mona Lisa face and silently stay above narrow perspectives before rallying any sides, knowing that your "freedom of choice" is heavily constrained. There is so much you can do: people you could have hit it off with perfectly in another setting could become your structural adversaries, while other employees you would have spontaneously dismissed as possible friends outside the institution could become your closest allies. Observation shouldn't be too naïvely empirical because things are rarely "what they seem", as sociologist Peter Berger underlined (Berger, 1963). Time will usually tell though. You also want to sense the atmosphere by looking at the way people interact (formal and to the point, overly familiar, tone, volume, degree of eye contact), at dressing and grooming code, at the decoration, the way objects are arranged (orderly, cluttered, etc.). Some events will incite you to loosen up but beware of "casual Friday" type traps if you are evolving in a corporate setting where management can use those kinds of tricks to make people come out of character. During the first day, you will probably be overwhelmed by information ("cognitive overload" state), so it is clever to find ways to remember names and information, such as taking phony bathroom breaks (not too many) to note things down. People will generally be obliging at first, especially in corporate cultures that tend to be relatively friendly such as the North American ones. But patience can sooner than later turn into friendly admonishment, light sarcasm, and cold remonstrance.

Step 8. Interpreting the data

All your observations won't be instantly intelligible, and you might never comprehend some of them. This is generally disturbing and can potentially be painful. As one of the world's leading group psychoanalysis theorists René Kaës deeply noticed, suffering inside institutions can, not only come from apprehensible sources, but also from not understanding the cause, the object, or the meaning of the suffering (Kaës, 2000). If analysis remains unproductive, we recommend letting go of unanswered questions to avoid rumination or overinterpretation (*"What did she mean?"*, *"Why did he say that?"*, *"Why has John been acting icy since day one?"*, *"What's going on here?"*, etc.). That being said, most things fall into place with time. As emphasized above, human problems involve many factors, and relying on common sense or only one action theory won't get you far. The *Fulatune* method proposes to interpret human phenomena from different levels and perspectives while avoiding unifactorial and moralistic judgments in terms of merits and vices because they usually lead to tautological explanations, such as *"she did good because she's a nice person"* or *"he messed up because he's stupid"*. For example, many reasons why parents can have a hard time parenting can be overlooked, especially in TV debates using "applause" signs monitored by some distracted technician. To adequately interpret parenting issues, one needs to take into account many factors, such as the historical development of human and children's rights, the confusing alternation of pedagogical models and trends, the scope of parental public services and family network, the neighborhood crime rate, the intelligence degree of TV programs, movies, and video games, the geographical region you live in (Scandinavia, Central America, etc.), the parent's own upbringing, desired or unwanted childbearing, income, economic inequalities, personality type, age and temperament of the child (and parent), Big pharma strategies and opioid epidemics, etc. In this particular case, recognizing the multiplicity of factors can help to discriminate what you can control from what's out of reach, and therefore set realistic objectives and plans. From an emotional point of view, careful interpretation can also lift some guilt on overwhelmed parents and generate more insight concerning "responsibilities", which are also collective.

Step 9. Revising the situation and problem

With some grip on probable causal factors and obstacles, it can be useful to reevaluate the situation and problem. After a few days or weeks, the question: *"How to become relatively efficient and fit in as well as possible without becoming a flunky or a pariah?"* can be revised and answered more precisely. Perhaps Isabella and Derrell now appear to be good role models to mimic for skill strengthening. You might also realize that "fitting in" is going to be a little more challenging than expected, leading to new questions, such as: *"To what extent am I willing to play the game?"*, *"The alpha male strategy seems to become counterproductive; perhaps it's best to stir away from it before it's too late?"*, *"Do I pretend I'm a vegan* (or carnivore) *too"?*, *"To display my adherence to this apparently cool corporate culture, should I also organize work reunions in my bedroom as Steve does ?"*, etc. Preliminary assessments might also have suggested that you can securely express your personality in the fantastically open-minded context, or that the use of hypercorrect diction is not necessary after all in this firm or NGO.

Step 10. Creating options

The *Fulatune* method proposes a particular way to write down ideas and answer questions. Teaching people to formulate accurate problems and solutions made it clear that trying to directly answer written questions without reworking them wasn't the best solution. To illustrate this point, we can compare two procedures:

a) trying to directly address the question

b) Decomposing the question and remodeling it

Say you try to directly answer the already formulated question:

"How to become relatively efficient and fit in as well as possible without becoming a flunky or a pariah?"

Quickly, after a blank moment, ideas might start to collide with each other. However, since they are dependent on many factors and issues, a state of cognitive overload might occur, even if highly trained in problem-solving.

We suggest reframing and decomposing: reformulate the question in the form of an affirmation and break it down into manageable parts to fill in gaps, but without yet trying to evaluate or rank the answers (eliminating, organizing and ranking comes later).

For example (these ideas are illustrative, not specific recommendations):

"The best way to becoming efficient could be to":

- Identify the most skillful employees
- Ask permission to observe them

- List and ask questions
- Take two extra hours a week of free time to read about techniques during the first month

"Fitting in without becoming a flunky could be done the following ways":

- Observe like an anthropologist and act like the locals for a while
- Don't smile all the time (they might expect you to do it forever)
- Try to master your facial (micro)expressions
- Accept all demands the first week but do politely let know some are taking time over primary tasks
- Gradually decrease requests for help after one or two weeks
- Decide what staff demands will be off limits and prepare excellent excuses if trespassing occurs

"Avoiding to the become a pariah could be done by":

- Avoiding over-demonstrating envy-generating skillfulness (if any)
- Being discreet about authority approval-seeking behaviors
- Resisting the temptation to correct others (yet) if you see a mistake or believe there is a more efficient way of doing something
- not appearing over-zealous (to your colleagues)
- etc.

The transformation of an interrogation into an affirmation allows your mind to focus on one action at a time. You can add "do's" and "don'ts" columns if helpful. The answers represent possible solutions units.

Everybody understands the word "solution". However, a solution is often preconceived as effective. For example, if you have 15 minutes in front of you, efficient "relaxing" can be achieved by ingesting one or two units of alcohol or by meditating. After consideration, meditating could appear like the most effective solution (no suspicious dragon breath, no psychomotor disturbances, no delayed "wiped out" side-effect, no unnecessary expense, no bad coping habit fostering, etc.). This is partly why researchers have distinguished two constructs: "solution" and "effective solution".

In social problem-solving research, a solution is:

"a situation-specific coping response or response pattern (cognitive or behavioral) that is the product or outcome of the problem-solving process when it is applied to a specific problematic situation." (D'Zurilla et al., 2004, p. 13).

But an effective solution is:

"one that achieves the problem-solving goal (i.e., changing the situation for the better or reducing the emotional distress that it produces), while at the same time maximizing other positive consequences and minimizing negative consequences. The relevant consequences include both personal and social outcomes, long-term

as well as short-term. With specific reference to an interpersonal problem, an effective solution is one that resolves the conflict or dispute by providing an outcome that is acceptable or satisfactory to all parties involved. This outcome may involve a consensus, compromise, or negotiated agreement that accommodates the interests and well-being of all concerned parties". (p. 13).

These definitions represent good signposts to go back to regularly during the decision-making process.

Step 11. Decision-making

Decision-making can start with eliminating ideas that now appear as relatively weak or ineffective. Then, each remaining option can be evaluated in terms of effectiveness, feasibility, and consequences for oneself and others. According to the characteristics of the options, it is often necessary to select criteria and associating coefficients (like in high school, to distinguish the relative weight of subjects like mathematics or civics). If you are thinking about switching jobs, you will have to deal with questions such as feasibility, income, necessity of retraining, relocation, deep desire, prestige, security, stress, self-esteem, weekly hours, core values, effects on partner or children, commuting time or gas expense, insurance coverage, probability of getting along with the new colleagues (Army, GAFA, IRS, Wall Street, McDonald's, etc.), general tolerance to hierarchy, starting capital, hard and soft skills, market state, etc. Will you rank prestige and self-esteem before starting capital, like "clients" who enrage badly trained social workers by imprudently pulling out a recent Californian smartphone during an interview? Or will you prefer an old-school one from Illinois because all that really matters to you is speaking truth to power? This rational process is sometimes draining, so it is preferable to have a thinking space and take breaks because decision-making can take days or weeks.

Step 12. Generating a solution plan

A solution plan implies the sequencing of the idea or ideas into steps. A solution can be simple or complex. A simple solution involves engaging in a goal-orientated behavior. But in most cases, solution plans to adapt cognitively, emotionally, and socially to complex environments require complex strategies. They can combine more than two solutions and/ or unfold into "contingency" plans with different scenarios (B, C, D) to be implemented according to the success or failure of plan A (Nezu et al., 2012). Having backup plans is not only wise, but it also reduces anxiety by reassuring the subject that possible failures will only be partial and temporary. Creating a solution plan implies organizing the chosen actions in time. Therefore, a timeline can be used to visually sequence behaviors. It also helps to decrease pressure by highlighting the fact that not everything needs to be done on the same day, week, or month. Generating efficient solution plans often requires initiation and practice. But it gets easier.

Step 13. Preparing to execute the plan

Since acting out the behaviors requested by the solution plan can be overwhelming, it is occasionally profitable to visualize the enactment, so that the physiological system can get progressively used to the emotional arousal caused by the imagined future event (tournament, interview, negotiation, "*we-need-to-talk*" invitation). It is often a smart idea to visualize or behaviorally rehearse the sequence while monitoring elements so that you can forget about controlling them in the midst of action (voice control, hand positioning, facial expression, wrestling feint-and-throw move, snappy answers, leave-taking, etc.). Many people avoid this phase because of its unpleasantness. But confronting it usually helps later.

Step 14. Enacting the solution plan

This is the moment of truth. You are now already halfway adapted to the situation. So, you should feel rather confident that you are moving in the right direction. You can be surprised at how serene you finally are, and even experience a state close to "flow" during action. But most of the time though, you will just reach stages without entering flow states. This shouldn't make you forget to notice those milestones and enjoy attaining them. Because neglecting to do so can trivialize objective accomplishments and tax your motivation. Some cultures take hard and deserving work for granted, which can be very tough on morale and self-esteem, especially for young children. Some talented stand-up comedians have addressed this occasionally tragic question with humor. In others, like the American one, encouraging expressions are unreluctantly used, such as *"well done"*, *"good job"*, or *"give yourself a round of applause"*.

Step 15. Monitoring, adjusting, and self-rewarding

This is why monitoring progress and rewarding yourself is usually considered healthy and helpful. There is definitely a North American twist to self-rewarding discourses, but this trait doesn't seem harmful unless it turns into excessive and unmerited gratification. It gets dopamine flowing and helps to carry on a possibly long and hard path to adaptation. Some steps in the adaptation process can be considered small and successful adjustments. For example, winning small or big championships over and over again can reinforce stress management skills and self-efficacy. One can only imagine how adapted and confident boxer Julio César Chávez was in the early 1990s with 89 wins and… 0 losses (Berger, 1994).

Step 16. Debriefing, recording the lessons, and recovering

Stepping back and retrospectively analyzing is important too because balanced feedback can avoid future sloppiness and enhance excellence by attuning even more sharply to environments that are rarely totally static. Recovering for a few days is also fundamental. More than physical rest, it includes elements such as psychological detachment, mental relaxation, and control over the environment (schedule, tasks, requests, etc.) (Bennett et al., 2018).

The *Fulatune* Steps to Clear-eyed Hardiness

Step 1. Setting up a thinking space

Step 2. Working on your "problem orientation"

Step 3. Consolidating biopsychosocial foundations

Step 4. Depicting the situation

Step 5. Defining the problem

Step 6. Raising preliminary goals and questions

Step 7. Observing and collecting data

Step 8. Interpreting the data

Step 9. Revising the situation and problem

Step 10. Creating options

Step 11. Decision-making

Step 12. Generating a solution plan

Step 13. Preparing to execute the plan

Step 14. Enacting the solution plan

Step 15. Monitoring, adjusting, and self-rewarding

Step 16. Debriefing, recording the lessons, and recovering

This chapter covered the main principles of the *Fulatune* method. In the face of complexity and uncertainty, the confusion attached to loads of possibilities often makes it necessary to go back to safe fundamentals. Contrarily to vague, ideological, or esoteric systems, the *Fulatune* method comes with an explanation of how adaptation concretely operates. It also proposes a set of steps meant to represent a guideline for progressive solution implementation. While a structured blueprint can be helpful at first, a looser approach can be developed with time and practice.

Table 1. *Synthetic table of the* Fulatune *hardiness training method*

Onset →	Processes →	Outcomes
-Ignorance **-Naïveté** **-Misinformation** **-Self-deception** **-Mystification**	-Reconsideration (acknowledging partial or total ignorance, recognizing possible misconceptions) -Disenchantment and acceptance -Learning (theoretically or the "hard way") -Analytical thinking skills acquisition -Practice, experience	**-Worldliness** **-Discernment** **-Acumen** **-Lucidity** ↑
-Maladaptation **-Insufficiency** **-Discrepancy** **-« Imposter syndrome »**	-Resource acquisition (nutritional, technical, financial, emotional) -Preparation (anticipation, rehearsal) -Practice (trial and error repetition) -Acculturation, socialization -Habituation, conditioning, desensitization, -Relaxation, recovery	**-Adaptation** **-Attunement** ↓
-Anxiety **-Stress**	-Feedback analysis -Progress and strengths awareness and monitoring -Self-efficacy development -Self-regulation improvement	**-Composure** **-Serenity** **-Charisma**

CHAPTER 6
Application and Topics

ༀ

The *Fulatune* foundations, procedures, and methods are designed as thinking tools and practical guidelines. However, their final purpose is of course to be applied to general and specific target issues across various settings. Below are listed non-exhaustive areas of application with practical examples.

Deep Insight

Insight is defined by the Merriam-Webster dictionary as a) *"the power or act of seeing into a situation"* and b) *"the act or result of apprehending the inner nature of things or of seeing intuitively"* (Merriam-Webster, n.d.). The *Fulatune* method enables readers to understand behaviors and situations with more discernment. It contributes to forming wiser judgments, making better decisions, and enhancing one's well-being as well as the ones of others. Developing insight particularly relies on the first two steps: observation and understanding. Readers can develop assessment skills by better understanding how a) perceptions are commonly biased, b) behaviors tend to be shaped, and c) situations can be determined. The method is especially suited for people dealing with complex situations involving many causes, viewpoints, and possible outcomes.

Specific Preparation

The *Fulatune* method can help prepare readers for specific and time-limited events. Combined with cognitive and behavioral techniques such as anticipation, visualization, rehearsal, relaxation, and voice and body-language monitoring, it is useful for optimally meeting demands in professional interviews, presentations, public speaking, negotiations, summons, or "*we-need-to-talk*" warnings.

Specific Long-Term Adaptation

Occasionally, one needs to prepare for a durable situation rather than a singular event. People don't always want to adapt, sometimes they just need to. If the reader is willing or needs to acculturate or more superficially adapt to a sturdy microcosm, the *Fulatune* method will help by providing hardiness tools. It is suitable for a long-term social commitment or obligation such as integrating a new company, an organization (educational, governmental, medical), a "total institution[11]" (Goffman, 1961) – like a

---

11   This concept was coined by Erving Goffman in his book *Asylums* (1961) to "*analyse a range of institutions in which whole blocks of people are bureaucratically processed, whilst being physically isolated from the normal round of activities, by being required to sleep, work, and play within the confines of the same institution*" (Scott, 2014, p. 763).

carceral, geriatric, or monastic establishment – or moving to a new neighborhood, city, or country.

Morning Routines: *Fulatune* style

Most advertised "morning routines" are uniform and invariable, as if there were no differences between working days and non-working days, between hard times and better times. Given that circumstances change, we suggest a variation of routines for working days, off days, ordinary times, and hard times. One doesn't have the same amount of time every morning either. During hardship, it is necessary to find more time to maintain one's mood and prevent it from going under due to pressure and crushing adversity. The *Fulatune* method can help people who wish to create one or more morning routines, who are partly unsatisfied with their own (spontaneous or not), or who believe a trouble-shooting session might be beneficial (is such or such element realistic, necessary, absent?). It conveys scientific information, cognitive and behavioral tips as well as principles to rank activities since the order in which they are executed matters.

Stress-Management: *Fulatune* style

The *Fulatune* method helps build global lifestyle strategies and timely tactical plans. It incorporates classic and original stress-management techniques as well as gradual exposure procedures that tend to generate physiological, cognitive, and emotional adaptations to stress, leading to composed behavior in the thick of it. One of the core ideas here is that if a baseline is overall respected, it will serve as a shock absorber, not *if*, but *when* push comes to shove. "Sunday evening" doesn't care to bother you with an upstairs neighbor leak or a child's broken arm. Timely tactical plans involve keeping a dormant expectative attitude so that you won't, at crunch time, scream irrational phrases such as *"Not now!"*, *"Not again!"* or *"This can't be happening!"*.

Endurance for Hard Times

Extremely difficult life episodes characterized by one or more very challenging problems do occur. In general, heavy situations tend to trigger cognitive distortions, negative emotions, defense mechanisms, hormonal changes (rise in cortisol levels for example), symptoms like irritability, or syndromes such as depression, etc. Psychologists and psychiatrists tend to distinguish between adaptive and maladaptive coping responses. Of course, overdrinking might soothe the pain, the anxiety, or the loneliness, but it will make things worse in the long run. Nevertheless, pragmatist professionals who have worked with addicts know that recommending substance abstinence at certain times is as ineffective as a priest asking a South American street kid to just "stop" snatching chains downtown or sniffing glue. Minimal external and internal conditions need to be met to initiate positive changes. The *Fulatune* method helps readers to understand as objectively as possible the situation, to distinguish factors that can be acted upon (retraining, picking up meditation, etc.) from the less manageable ones (other people's attitudes and behaviors) as well as the ones that are simply out of control such as "large processes" (Tilly, 1989) (deindustrialization, globalization, international drugs circulation, etc.). While it supports the formulation of emotion-focused and problem-focused coping responses as well as effective solution plans, it also teaches classic and original coping tips to endure the situation, maintain morale, and just keep walking, step by step, until the problem is partially or totally solved.

Global 3D Development

The *Fulatune* method can be aimed at developing knowledge and skills from a truly holistic perspective. While the state of hyper-specialization attained by modern societies simply makes it no longer possible to master as many skills as, say, Leonardo da Vinci in the 15th and 16th centuries, it is nevertheless possible to counter the tendency to focus solely on the development of one-sided skills (fitness without culture, communication without substance, observation without framework, art without imagination, politics without conviction, beautifying without kindness, influencing without benevolence, managing without humanism, etc.). Often, many people invest a lot of time, energy, and money in an activity that becomes a cornerstone in self-esteem regulation (silhouette shaping, skincare, styling, gaming, intellectualizing, child-raising, etc.). However, psychologists working on rumination such as Susan Nolen-Hoeksema have come to notice that not having a diversity of gratification sources (Law, 2005) can lead to rumination symptoms. On a broader level, being only agreeable to watch, skilled in finance, or good at video games will generate downsides: you might end up suffering from being considered uneducated, austere, or immature. And what will you have left if the basket in which all your eggs are put gets crushed? The *Fulatune* method doesn't deliver instrumental and standardized "general culture" syllabuses but rather encourages knowledge acquisition, skills diversification, and cultural openness. It can assist in developing composure with evidence-based nutritional psychology and relaxation techniques, interpersonal and public communication skill-building, fitness and self-defense general rules (physical self-confidence can be a transposable skill and an element of charisma), as well as tailored sociology-based demeanor and attire counseling for specific context attunement.

More information on the *Fulatune* applications is available on www.3dworldly.com

CONCLUSION

❧

Grounded in the observation of contemporary trends assigned to mainstream technologies of the self, this primer intended to discuss important flaws and obstacles to satisfactory interpretation and adaptation processes. It presented original foundations, principles, and steps to better control perception biases, attune effectively to endured or sought-after environments, and stay composed in the face of adversity or danger. The multidisciplinary rationale was meant to be brief, but sufficiently detailed for readers to know why the method was conceived that way and not otherwise. Along with the precept according to which readers deserve more consideration than simply being expected to take assertions for granted, a comprehensive description of the 16 steps was chosen to serve as a precise procedural guide. Specificity was chosen over generality since it is often easier to exclude a known element than to include an unknown component. Some learners favor elaborate recommendations, others, overall suggestions. Feel free to use the handbook according to your inclinations. May this work not only help you cope more skillfully with life but also convey to you the vitality to lend a hand to others.

BIBLIOGRAPHY

ↄ

Books and articles, dictionary entries, and other works

Books and articles

American Psychological Association. (2022, December 1). What you need to know about willpower: The psychological science of self-control. https://www.apa.org/topics/personality/willpower.

Arena, A. F., Mobbs, S., Sanatkar, S., Williams, D., Collins, D., Harris, M., Harvey, S. B., & Deady, M. (2023). Mental health and unemployment: A systematic review and meta-analysis of interventions to improve depression and anxiety outcomes. *Journal of Affective Disorders, 335*, 450-472.

Ash, M. G. (1998). *Gestalt psychology in German culture, 1890-1967: Holism and the quest for objectivity.* Cambridge University Press.

Austin, J. L. (1976). *Sense and Sensibilia.* Oxford University Press.

Backhouse, R. E., & Fontaine, P. (2012). *The history of the social sciences since 1945.* Cambridge University Press.

Baron, J. (2007). *Thinking and Deciding* (4th ed.). Cambridge University Press.

Basu, S. (2006). *Spy princess: The life of Noor Inayat Khan.* History Press.

Baumeister, R. F., & Tierney, J. (2011). *Willpower: Rediscovering the greatest human strength.* Penguin Putnam.

Bennett, A. A., Bakker, A. B., & Field, J. G. (2018). Recovery from work-related effort: A meta-analysis. *Journal of Organizational Behavior, 39*(3), 262-275.

Berger, P. (1994, January 30). Chavez suffers 1st loss. *Washington Post (Washington, D.C.: 1974).* https://www.washingtonpost.com/archive/sports/1994/01/30/chavez-suffers-1st-loss/f3fb2d4c-4c23-48ae-a9d6-53019b72d76c/

Berger, P. L. (1963). *Invitation to sociology: A humanistic perspective.* Anchor Books.

Bergson, H. (1972). Message au Congrès Descartes (1937). In A. Robinet (Ed.), *Mélanges* (pp. 1574-1579). Presses Universitaires de France (PUF).

Bocquet, C. (2002). Biological Adaptation. In *Encyclopedia Universalis.* (pp. 244-247). Cited in Simonet, G. (2010). *The concept of adaptation: Interdisciplinary scope and involvement in climate change. Sapiens, 3*(1), 1-9.

Bourdieu, P. (1985). *Bourdieu: Distinction : A social critique of the judgment of taste.* Harvard University Press.

Bourdieu, Pierre. (2000). *Pascalian Meditations.* Stanford University Press.

Bursztyn, L., Egorov, G., Haaland, I., Rao, A., & Roth, C. (2022). Scapegoating during crises. *AEA Papers and Proceedings. American Economic Association, 112,* 151-155.

Claims Conference. (2020, August 13). *First-ever 50-state survey on holocaust knowledge of American millennials and Gen Z reveals shocking results.* Claims Conference. https://www.claimscon.org/millennial-study/

Clay, C. (2003-2004). *SAS Survival Secrets.* BBC Bristol. https://collections-search. bfi.org.uk/web/Details/ ChoiceFilmWorks/150680298

Cohen, I. (2006). Habitus and field. In B. S. Turner (Ed.), *The Cambridge Dictionary of Sociology* (p. 259). Cambridge University Press.

Crockett, Z. (2019, November 23). *The tragic data behind Black Friday deaths.* The Hustle. https://thehustle.co/black-friday-deaths-injuries-data/

d'Addio, A., & d'Ercole, M. M. (2005). *Trends and determinants of fertility rates: The role of policies* (OECD social, employment and migration working papers), vol. 27, 91 p.

Das, S. S., & Pattanayak, S. (2023). Understanding the effect of leadership styles on employee well-being through leader-member exchange. *Current Psychology,* 42, 21310-21325.

de Beauvoir, S., & Sartre, J.-P. (2017). *La cérémonie des adieux / Entretiens avec Jean-Paul Sartre.* Editions Gallimard.

Debord, G. (1984). *Society of the spectacle.* Black & Red.

D'Zurilla, T. J., & Goldfried, M. R. (1971). Problem-solving and behavior modification. *Journal of Abnormal Psychology, 78*(1), 107-126.

D'Zurilla, T. J., Nezu, A. M., & Maydeu-Olivares, A. (2004). Social problem solving: Theory and assessment. In E. C. Chang, T. J. D'Zurilla, & L. J.

Sanna (Ed.), *Social problem solving: Theory, research, and training* (pp. 11-27). American Psychological Association.

Foucault, M. (1988). Technologies of the self. In L. H. Martin, H. Gutman, & P. H. Hutton (Eds.), *Technologies of the self: A seminar with Michel Foucault* (pp. 16–49). University of Massachusetts Press.

Herrnstein, R. J., & Murray, C. (1994). *The bell curve: Reshaping of American life by differences in intelligence.* Simon and Schuster.

Hobsbawm, E. (2020). *The age of extremes: 1914-1991.* Little, Brown Book Group.

Jansz, J., & Van Drunen, P. (Eds.). (2004). *A social history of psychology.* Blackwell Publishing.

Jones, M. D. (1998). *Thinker's Toolkit: 14 powerful techniques for problem-solving.* Times Books.

Kaës, R. (2000). Réalité psychique et souffrance dans les institutions. In R. Kaës (Ed.), *L'institution et les institutions: Études psychanalytiques* (pp. 1-46). Dunod.

Kobasa, S. C. (1979). Stressful life events, personality, and health: an inquiry into hardiness. *Journal of Personality and Social Psychology, 37*(1), 1-11.

Law, B. M. (2005, November 1). Probing the depression-rumination cycle. *Monitor on Psychology, 36*(10). https://www.apa.org/monitor/nov05/cycle

Lewin, K., Lippitt, R., & White, R. K. (1939). Patterns of aggressive behavior in experimentally created "social climates." *The Journal of Social Psychology, 10*(2), 269-299.

Lewin, K. (1951). *Field theory in social science: selected theoretical papers (Edited by Dorwin Cartwright.).* Harpers.

Louis, É. (2021). *Changer: méthode.* Editions du Seuil.

Masento, N. A., Golightly, M., Field, D. T., Butler, L. T., & van Reekum, C. M. (2014). Effects of hydration status on cognitive performance and mood. *The British Journal of Nutrition, 111*(10), 1841-1852.

Modin, Y., Deniau, J.-C., & Ziarek, A. (1994). *My five Cambridge friends.* Headline Book Publishing.

National Health Service. (2020, February 26). *Coping with fatigue.* NHS Inform. https://www.nhsinform.scot/care-support-and-rights/palliative-care/symptom-control/coping-with-fatigue

Nezu, A., & D'Zurilla, T. J. (1979). An experimental evaluation of the decision-making process in social problem-solving. *Cognitive Therapy and Research, 3*(3), 269-277.

Nezu, A. M., & Nezu, C. M. (2019). *Emotion-centered problem-solving therapy: Treatment guidelines.* Springer Publishing.

Nezu, A. M., Nezu, C. M., & D'Zurilla, T. J. (2012). *Problem-solving therapy: A treatment manual.* Springer Publishing.

Nossiter, A. (2019, December 20). 3 french executives convicted in suicides of 35 workers. *The New York Times.* https://www.nytimes.com/2019/12/20/world/europe/france-telecom-suicides.html

O'Kennedy, R. (2000). The immune system in sport: getting the balance right. *British Journal of Sports Medicine, 34*(3), 161.

Pickett, K., & Wilkinson, R. (2010). *The spirit level: Why equality is better for everyone.* Penguin Books.

Plato. (1914). *Euthyphro* (H. N. Fowler, Trans.). London, England: William Heinemann.

Robichaud, M., & Dugas, M. J. (2005). Negative problem orientation (Part I): psychometric properties of a new measure. *Behaviour Research and Therapy, 43*(3), 391-401.

Rose, N. (2012). *Inventing our selves: Psychology, power, and personhood.* Cambridge University Press.

Scheid, T. L., & Brown, T. N. (Eds.). (2012). *A handbook for the study of mental health: Social contexts, theories, and systems* (2nd ed.). Cambridge University Press.

Scott, J. (2014). Total institution. In J. Scott (Ed.), *A Dictionary of sociology* (p. 763). Oxford University Press.

Segal, N. L. (2013). Twin Studies [Data set]. In *Oxford Bibliographies Online Datasets.* Oxford University Press.

Sewell, W. H. (2005). *Logics of history: Social theory and social transformation.* University of Chicago Press.

Szczepanik, J. E., Brycz, H., Kleka, P., Fanslau, A., Zarate, C. A., Jr, & Nugent, A. C. (2020). Metacognition and emotion - How accurate perception of own biases relates to positive feelings and hedonic capacity. *Consciousness and Cognition, 82*(102936), 102936.

Thatcher, M. (1987, September 23). *Interview for Woman's Own ("no such thing [as society]")* (D. Keay, Interviewer) [Interview]. https://www.margaretthatcher.org/document/106689

Tilly, C. (1989). *Big structures, large processes, huge comparisons.* Russell Sage Foundation.

Tversky, A., & Kahneman, D. (1974). Judgment under uncertainty: Heuristics and biases: Biases in judgments reveal some heuristics of thinking under uncertainty. *Science (New York, N.Y.), 185*(4157), 1124-1131.

United Nations. (n.d.). 2021 Global Multidimensional Poverty Index (MPI). *Human Development Reports.* Retrieved November 21, 2023, from https://hdr.undp.org/content /2021-global-multidimensional-poverty-index-mpi

Wacquant, L. (2009). *Punishing the poor: The neoliberal government of social insecurity.* Duke University Press.

Wilkinson, R., & Pickett, K. (2009). *The spirit level: Why greater equality makes societies stronger.* Bloomsbury Publishing Plc.

Winsper, C., Bilgin, A., Thompson, A., Marwaha, S., Chanen, A. M., Singh, S. P., Wang, A., & Furtado, V. (2020). The prevalence of personality disorders in the community: a global systematic review and meta-analysis. *The British Journal of Psychiatry: The Journal of Mental Science, 216*(2), 69-78.

World Health Organization. (2022a). *Physical activity.* Who.int. https://www.who.int/news-room/fact-sheets/detail/ physical-activity

World Health Organization. (2022b). *World mental health report: transforming mental health for all.* https://iris.who.int/bitstream/handle/10665/356119/9789240049338-eng.pdf?sequence=1

Wouters, C. (2021). *Informalization: Manners and emotions since 1890.* SAGE Publications.

Zakaras, A. (2022). *The roots of American individualism: Political myth in the age of Jackson.* Princeton University Press.

Dictionary entries

American Psychological Association. (2023, November 11). Adaptive behavior. In *APA Dictionary of psychology*. Retrieved November 17, 2023, from https://dictionary.apa.org/adaptative-behavior

American Psychological Association. (2018, April 19). Adaptation. In *APA Dictionary of psychology*. Retrieved November 17, 2023, from https://dictionary.apa.org/adaptation

American Psychological Association. (2018, April 19). Adjustment process. In *APA Dictionary of psychology*. Retrieved November 17, 2023, from https://dictionary.apa.org/adjustment-process

American Psychological Association. (2018, April 19). Big Five personality model. In *APA Dictionary of psychology*. Retrieved November 17, 2023, from https://dictionary.apa.org/big-five-personality-model

American Psychological Association. (2018, April 19). Conscientiousness. In *APA Dictionary of psychology*. Retrieved November 17, 2023, from https://dictionary.apa.org/ conscientiousness

American Psychological Association. (2018, April 19). Epigenetics. In *APA Dictionary of psychology*. Retrieved November 17, 2023, from https://dictionary.apa.org/rationalization

American Psychological Association. (2018, April 19). Existential psychology. In *APA Dictionary of psychology*. Retrieved November 17, 2023, from https://dictionary.apa.org/ existential-psychology

American Psychological Association. (2018, April 19). Flow. In *APA Dictionary of psychology*. Retrieved November 17, 2023, from https://dictionary.apa.org/flow

American Psychological Association. (2018, April 19). Functionalism. In *APA Dictionary of psychology*. Retrieved November 17, 2023, from https://dictionary.apa.org/functionalism

American Psychological Association. (2018, April 19). Hardiness. In APA Dictionary of psychology (N.d.). Retrieved December 21, 2023, from https://dictionary.apa.org/hardiness

American Psychological Association. (2018, April 19). Learned helplessness. In *APA Dictionary of psychology*. Retrieved November 17, 2023, from https://dictionary.apa.org/learned-helplessness

American Psychological Association. (2018, April 19). Learning. In *APA Dictionary of psychology*. Retrieved November 17, 2023, from https://dictionary.apa.org/learning

American Psychological Association. (2018, April 19). Maladaptation. In *APA Dictionary of psychology*. Retrieved November 17, 2023, from https://dictionary.apa.org/maladaptation

American Psychological Association. (2018, April 19). Neuroticism. In *APA Dictionary of psychology*. Retrieved November 17, 2023, from https://dictionary.apa.org/neuroticism

American Psychological Association. (2023, November 17). Personality disorder. In *APA Dictionary of psychology*. *Retrieved November 17, 2023, from https://dictionary.apa.org/personality-disorder*

American Psychological Association. (2018, April 19). Rationalization. In *APA Dictionary of psychology*. Retrieved November 17, 2023, from https://dictionary.apa.org/rationalization

Merriam-Webster. (n.d.). Insight. In Merriam-webster.com. Retrieved November 22, 2023, from
https://www.merriam-webster.com/dictionary/insight

Merriam-Webster. (n.d.). Observation. In *Merriam-Webster.com dictionary*. Retrieved December 21, 2023, from https://www.merriam-webster.com/dictionary/observation

Merriam-Webster. (n.d.). Perspectivism. In *Merriam-Webster.com dictionary*. Retrieved November 22, 2023, from https://www.merriam-webster.com/dictionary/perspectivism

Merriam-Webster. (n.d.). Understanding. In *Merriam-Webster.com dictionary*. Retrieved December 21, 2023, from https://www.merriam-webster.com/dictionary/understanding

Other works: song

Valentine B. & Valentine, J. (1982). *Money's too tight*. Bridge records.

INDEX OF KEY CONCEPTS & AUTHORS

* 9 7 8 2 4 8 7 4 1 4 0 0 6 *